The New
Dictionary
of
Spiritual
Thought

The New
Dictionary
of
Spiritual
Thought

By
Carol E. Parrish-Harra

SPARROW HAWK PRESS
Tahlequah, Oklahoma

Library of Congress Cataloging-in-Publication Data
Parrish-Harra, Carol E.
The New Dictionary of Spiritual Thought
        A dictionary of 1,100 Western and Eastern esoteric and spiritual terms and concepts by Carol E. Parrish-Harra. Includes biographies, symbols, and illustrations.
        ISBN 0-94027-11-7: $14.95
        1. Spiritual dictionary. 2. Religion–Esoteric Christianity. 3. Western and Eastern spiritualist traditions and philosophical thought. 4. Agni Yoga teachings. 5. Kabalah. 6. Hermetic principles. 7. Buddhistic concepts. I. Title.

Library of Congress Catalog Card Number
93-087756

Manufactured in the United States of America

Dedicated to Sophia

I, Wisdom, have created prudence,
And I possess knowledge and reason.
I love those who love me;
And those who seek me shall find me.

Proverbs 8.12,17

Publisher's Note

This dictionary does much more than define terms unique to spiritual study. It enlightens its user with the concepts and mythology which gave rise to these terms. Use it as your faithful companion as you progress on the Path, and you will find it an indispensable key to understanding the esoteric wisdom of the ancients.

Prepared by the well respected mystic and Dean of Sancta Sophia Seminary, Carol E. Parrish-Harra, this exceptional compendium is the result of the author's pursuit of ageless wisdom teachings, a search which led her to a guru high in the Himalayas, to sacred sites in Peru, the USSR, Egypt, and the Orient, to the Gobi for Wesak, and to the Yucatan and Mexico for study of the Maya culture under the tutelage of the wisdomkeeper, Hunbatz Men, whose lineage as such predates Columbus.

Dean Parrish-Harra is a popular lecturer in many countries, including the United States and Russia. In 1981 she established a spiritual community in Tahlequah, Oklahoma, in the foothills of the Ozarks, now the home of Sancta Sophia Seminary, where she works tirelessly to disseminate the wisdom of the ancient teachings.

Other Works by Carol E. Parrish-Harra
The Book of Rituals – Personal and Planetary Transformation
The Aquarian Rosary – Reviving the Art of Mantra Yoga
Messengers of Hope
A New Age Handbook on Death and Dying

Acknowledgements

Certainly I wish to acknowledge the many people who have prompted me to define the words I have come to depend upon in order to share concepts and ideas that bring new awareness and peace of mind to many.

The first time someone said to me, "I need a dictionary if I'm going to hang out with you," I had no idea someday I would create one. But now I have, and to Grace Bradley who said it to me first, I say, "Thank you!"

My second thank you is to Mary Beth Marvin who has edited it for and with me. When I thought I could not answer one more question or define one more word, Mary Beth, in her fine journalistic manner, persisted. So the accomplishment belongs to us both. And I must add, I have loved creating this book; it has been as much fun as a jigsaw puzzle.

I would like to add my appreciation of Norma Hallstrom for her dedicated research and copyediting, and a very special thank you to Lucille Perry, my beloved secretary and coworker, who keeps things moving smoothly for me while I do these special things I love.

To the other members of our team who helped make this dictionary a reality, I am truly appreciative: John R. Eggen, Jr., Marketing Manager, Eliot Ricciardelli, Project Manager, and Marianne H. Sansing for her contributions to cover design, typesetting, and creative layout.

May these ideas and concepts bless the ones who explore them. May Light descend on Earth!

Carol E. Parrish-Harra

Editor's Notes

Because of their unique importance in esoteric teachings, Agni Yoga and Kabalah references are highlighted throughout the dictionary by the symbols of a flame and a tree of life, respectively.

A truly useful reference work must, by its very nature, reflect countless sources and authorities, both well-known and esoteric. We wish to express our particular indebtedness to *The Holy Bible from the Ancient Eastern Text,* George M. Lamsa's Aramaic translation from the Peshitta (A.J. Holman Company, 1933) for biblical references (unless otherwise noted) and *The Kybalion – A Study of the Hermetic Philosophy of Ancient Egypt and Greece,* by Three Initiates (Yogi Publication Society, 1912), an important source for the secret wisdom teachings said to have originated with Hermes Trismegistus. We are further indebted to these important references for biographical information: *Oxford Dictionary of the Christian Church* (Oxford University Press, 1974) and *Dictionary of Bible and Religion* (Abingdon Press, 1986).

In the interest of completeness and to encourage further study, relevant major literary works are cited at the end of biographical entries, while throughout the text, cross-referenced words and terms are designated by small capital letters.

A consistent effort has been made to avoid sexist terms and constructions where possible, without altering meaning or compromising grammatical usage.

Introduction

When I began to have meditation experiences, my mind would fill with concepts beyond my understanding. I would "know" something, but would have no words for the knowing. I struggled quietly. On occasion I would attempt to ask or share these promptings with others. I quickly learned my thoughts were not grasped by others and that I appeared foolish as I attempted to inquire about beyond-words notions.

Yet, the inner life persisted as I recalled the realizations that had come as I stood in the presence of the Light Being during my near-death experience. In that wondrous time, all things seemed so clear.

It would be several years before, in meditation, I would again touch the wisdom I felt was mine to share. In time, my quest led to wise teachers who would encourage and bless me as they shared their precious inner life and new understandings.

Recapitulation was a time of joy and delight–finding words for the knowingness. Each new concept brought new conviction to my spirit, giving form to the expanding mind map in the back of my head. In time I would be able to pass on to others the ancient and ageless truths that serve as light on the path. May they be as a lamp on your way.

Carol E. Parrish-Harra

Abstract Mind. The higher aspect of mind in which we contact conceptual thought, think in abstract terms, and formulate plans and purposes. The level of the mental plane from which come the impulses and purposes of the spirit in humanity. That which is created by the abstract mind eventually crystallizes into form and descends into concrete mind. The work of the fifth ROOT RACE is to develop the powers of abstract mind. *See* Concrete mind.

Abyss. A profound inner experience that occurs in the life of those who, seeking knowledge of God, penetrate beyond the realm of knowable things into the vast chasms of time and space. Also, the invisible and incomprehensible nature of God experienced as darkness or emptiness by the dedicated seeker during a "DARK NIGHT OF THE SOUL."

Active imagination. An exercise developed by Carl Jung as an aid to understanding personal symbology in a dream, meditation, etc. The dreamer imagines and describes orally or in writing a dialogue between self and a symbol or between two symbols.

Active meditation. A form of meditation in which the mind is poised and alert, rather than passive, focused upon a thought, word, or image. The practitioner intends to become magnetically charged with a SEED THOUGHT or an ideal to attract droplets of divine energy and wisdom or streams of creative ideas–to pierce through veils to the quality and essence of a thought. A "knowing" technique to penetrate and gain knowledge from the CLOUD OF KNOWABLE THINGS, the mind of God, or the higher storehouse of wisdom. Subtle concepts contained within a chosen thought-form rush into the mind prepared to receive these energies. Active meditation is recommended after developing a receptive consciousness–an open and ready mind.

❦ **Actualism.** A school of ESOTERIC thought derived from AGNI YOGA teachings. Russell Paul Schofield, writer, poet, and teacher, established a number of Schools of Actualism across the United States to bring about the realization that "humanity must free itself, at all levels of consciousness, from image-mechanism manipulation, so that every member of the human family may express his or her Actual Self creatively." *Imprint Unmistakable,* 1969.

Acupressure. A defined system of use of pressure exerted on specific points of the body for balancing or stimulating the energy flow of the ETHERIC BODY in health-supportive ways.

Acupuncture. A system using a variety of needles on specific points of the body for balancing or stimulating the energy flow of the etheric body in health-supportive ways.

Adam Kadmon. The archetypal wo/man, according to the Kabalah. In the Christian tradition, "heavenly man" or the "mystical body of Christ wherein we are all one."

Adept. An OCCULT degree or Soul-realized being working on laws of inner reality. Divided into two classes: one to demonstrate outward use of inner forces in human life and consciousness; the other to create reservoirs of energy to sustain forces of nature, direction of ELEMENTALS, etc., to support outer manifestation.

Adoration. One of the important practices of Christianity for the PURIFICATION of the astral body. Adoration guides the process of emotion to devotion, then devotion to adoration to lift the emotional focus to the highest levels of the astral reality. Through the power of ASPIRATION, we connect with our inner guidance. The archetypes, deities, and saints we hold in adoration link us to energies of the higher realities at this level of the ASTRAL PLANE. The passion of adoration purifies.

Advent. This beginning of the Christian year includes four Sundays before Christmas day. During this time, we look forward to celebrating Jesus' birth. We do this by thinking about our lives and trying to live up to God's plan for us. Purple, the color of the season, shows we are sorry for what we have done wrong and asks forgiveness. An Advent wreath–four candles on a green wreath (light one at a time on the four Sundays)–is symbolic of this season.

Affirmation. A statement used repeatedly to program the basic nature to a new reality. A tool for making change, for reprogramming the conscious mind. One of the mental disciplines.

Agapé. A love bond spiritual in nature – usually understood as the unconditional love of soul for soul. Also, the love of God for humanity. The spontaneous, self-giving love expressed freely without calculation of cost or gain to the giver or merit to the receiver. Christian love in its highest manifestation held as a goal for humanity.

Age of Flowers. The name the Maya give to the forthcoming era, also generally known as the Aquarian Age or Golden Age of Enlightenment.

Ageless wisdom. The hidden wisdom – veiled by materialistic and rational thinking – that underlies all religions and cultures. Includes folk wisdom, archetypes, myths, and allegories that seek to explain the mysteries of life.

Ageless wisdom teachings (also called mystery, ancient wisdom, or esoteric teachings). These teachings have been preserved traditionally for those deemed ready by a knowledgeable one who passes the teachings on and, by doing so, accepts a karmic responsibility.

Agni Invisibilae. The bioelectric energy which enters and acts upon the body of one attuned to the higher realities, seeking to purify and illumine the consciousness. These invisible energies of transcendence are symbolized as a fire of purification and illumination igniting the divine potential within and clear the mental and emotional bodies of GLAMOURS and ILLUSIONS, "burning away" distorted THOUGHTFORMS. Agni Invisibilae, as these higher energies are called in the Agni Yoga teachings, correlate to similar terms of other spiritual traditions. This fire, released into individual lives, cleanses with a discriminating fiery force–similar to the experience of PENTECOST.

Agni Yoga – An Introduction

Because Agni Yoga often uses terms in a slightly different way, Agni terms are specifically designated throughout the dictionary. Agni Yoga writings were received by transmission through the Russian Christian mystics, Helena and Nicholas Roerich, so when translated from Russian to English, the terms convey a unique meaning. Agni terms, virtues, and themes propose guidelines, rather than rigid dogma for attaining an ethical life. Special note is made of them by the symbol of a flame.

When NICHOLAS ROERICH designed the Banner of Peace, introducing it to the world in 1929, he stated that the three red disks – encircled by a red ring on a field of white – represent art, science, and religion. Through a synthesis of these three, culture can unite humanity in peace.

Art is a science when we are able to define the discipline, the structure, and the controllability within set boundaries.

Science is an art when its creativity and true purpose of experimentation are allowed to flow and be acknowledged.

Religion can be practiced as both an art and a science, as well as a path of devotion. The true purpose of religion is to realign us with the source of life. When we worship God following a defined format of commandments, dogmas, and practices (either inner or outer), we utilize the collective power of the religion to assist us in the ascent. Our theology must support and sustain us in our journey toward spirituality.

Banner of Peace

An ignorant person must be civilized first of all, then educated, after which he becomes intelligent. Then comes refinement and realization of synthesis, which is crowned by the acceptance of the idea of culture. Not a single narrow specialist, no matter how high his professional skill, can be considered a cultural leader. Culture is synthesis. Culture knows and understands the foundations of life and creativeness, because it is the cult of worship or reverence for the creative fire, which is life.

–Nicholas Roerich

Agni Yoga. *See* Yoga; *and page 4.*

Agni, Lord of Fire. A Hindu God. A reference from the *Vedas* that correlates with the concept of "Our God is a fiery God."

Agnostic. A person of any heritage who questions dogma and defined teachings, considering him- or herself a freethinker and reserving the right to examine independently.

Agnus Dei. Latin for "Lamb of God," a favorite and familiar symbol of Jesus Christ. John 1.29 records, "Behold the Lamb of God, who takes away the sins of the world." When depicted with a banner, the lamb symbolizes Christ's victory over death.

Aha. This common expression refers to insights and realizations that come in a perceptive moment of integration. When certain barriers in the psychological nature dissolve, bits and pieces of life shift and blend rapidly before the mind's eye–an "aha." An interesting aside: For an experience to become an aha, it must register or resound to something within us; therefore, the knowledge or revelation must become conscious and impact our awareness.

Ahura Mazda. The name of God in the ZOROASTRIAN tradition, also called Ormazd.

Ain, Ain Soph, Ain Soph Aur. Kabalistic terms for the very source of life acknowledging the limitless nature of the Creator. From this point, "about which naught can be known," divine Mind emanates its mysteries through four worlds, or levels of vibration, into the world of creation as we know it. Depicted as three partial circles above the kabalistic TREE OF LIFE.

Aïvanhov, Omraam Mikhael. b. Bulgaria, 1900, d. 1986. Prolific writer, teacher, and seer. He gave to his followers a set of teachings called Surya or SOLAR YOGA, the Yoga of the Sun, believing that we draw our energies from the Christ who dwells in the Sun. His followers practice a discipline of witnessing the sunrise to meditate and pray so that they may live their lives in daily harmony and find the courage and will to transform themselves. A scholar well grounded in the physical sciences, he taught that all natural laws and phenomena are translations on the physical plane of those existing on the spiritual plane. His visions of God led him to "choose the path of light, the path of selflessness and sacrifice, because God who is all those things is also the greatest and most perfect beauty....With divine knowledge, you can never be the same; as soon as you know even a

5

few aspects of the truth, you are transformed, and are capable of helping others." He envisioned the center of the Earth to be a hollow region called Agartha, inhabited by an advanced race of beings with a utopian political system. These Agartheans, concerned about humanity, are the alien visitors reported widely as UFOs. His teachings are preserved in 300 volumes of lectures. *The Second Birth,* 1976.

Ajna. The Sanskrit term for "brow center." *See* Chakras.

Aka cord. The etheric bond or psychic energy that remains attached to another after touch occurs between the two. This cord carries emotions and thoughts over an invisible connection for a period as long as emotion keeps it energized. Often used to direct healing to another at a distance. The term is derived from the Huna tradition.

Akashic records. The chronicle of events mentally and emotionally imprinted on the reflective ethers of the Earth and held as individual and group memory in all planetary life. The etheric level records or reflects a living chronicle of life, the story of the planetary being.

Alchemy. The TRANSMUTATION of one substance into another (as in turning base metals into gold),

symbolic of the transmutation of matter into spirit that causes a new birth (through regeneration) within the individual."Be ye transformed by the renewing of your mind." A process by which the ego extracts the "conscious soul" or ultimate spiritual essence through life experiences while in the physical body. An earlier term was *magick,* later *alchemy* came into use, and today we say *transformation.*

Alder, Vera Stanley. b. England, 1898, d. 1984. The author of seven books on esoteric teachings, translated worldwide into numerous languages. An original member of the Discipleship in the New Age, a group taught by MASTER DJWHAL KHUL, the communicant of ALICE BAILEY. She almost single-handedly maintained the Order of World Guardians from her private office. Alder was recognized as having "a rare gift for synthesizing the essentials of esoteric teachings." *The Finding of the Third Eye,* 1938; *The Initiation of the World,* 1939; *From the Mundane to the Magnificent,* 1979.

Alignment. Attuned to, on a wave length with, working in consort with.

Allah. The name for "the one God" from the Islamic tradition.

"All is ready, Master. Come." A special chant used at Wesak celebration but most significant as we stand ready to receive great outpourings of grace.

Aloha. This familiar Hawaiian greeting literally conveys, "I salute the divine presence within you," *Alo* meaning "presence" and *ha* meaning "divine breath" (as it does in Hindi). This salutation holds the same concept as NAMASTÉ.

Alpha and Omega. As the first and last characters in the Greek alphabet, these letters symbolize totality in the One, in whom creation began and by whom it will end. To Christians, it represents the omnipresence of Christ.

Altered state. Any state of consciousness differing from the typical.

Altruism. An awareness closely related to unconditional love expressed as unconditional giving, "no strings attached."

Amanuensis. A person who takes dictation and/or functions almost as a servant to an authority. In spiritual thought, one who receives the messages dictated by a holy one (note the *manu* portion of the word)–usually a teacher in spirit – and becomes the outerworld representative. Examples from the esoteric tradition are ALICE A. BAILEY for MASTER DJWHAL KHUL and HELENA ROERICH for MASTER MORYA.

Anchor. The source for this Christian symbol of hope and steadfastness is Hebrews 6.19: "That promise is like an anchor to us; it upholds the soul so that it may not be shaken, and it penetrates beyond the veil of the temple." Anchors are found in many inscriptions in the catacombs of Rome. They were often carved on old Christian gems.

Ancient wisdom. *See* Ageless wisdom.

Androgyny. The balance of masculine and feminine qualities within a personality.

Angel of the presence. The soul potential waiting behind the DWELLER ON THE THRESHOLD to express as the awareness of the mature soul.

Angelic kingdom. The kingdom of the angelic hosts, known in the East as the kingdom of the DEVAS, or "the Shining Ones." These active, creative form-builders of objective creation are in ceaseless action as directors and designers, artists and producers. The personifi-

7

cations associated with angelic beings are not to be regarded as dense realities but rather as parts of a parallel kingdom on its own path of evolution dwelling in the astral with the densest manifestation in the etheric realm. These physically invisible but omnipresent intelligences – from nature spirits to archangels – bring divine thought into form without intervention of individuality. The angelic kingdom – parallel to the human kingdom – is an intelligent lifestream in charge of life principles.

Angels. The word angel is derived from the Greek word *angelos* and means "messenger." Also known as devic evolution, an analogous family which evolves parallel to humanity upon planet Earth. The densest level they inhabit is the astral. The Christ is teacher of angels and humanity, with similar levels of initiation. Angels are celestial rulers of Aquarius. Mother Mary, a Master, or advanced one in this family, is known as Queen of Heaven and of Earth.

Anger. As a barrier to spiritual growth, anger is an ego creation of distorted astral energy that seems a natural reaction to threat. Neither bad nor good, it is an emotional reaction that generates power with which to defend and protect the ego, or nonself. Anger/distorted emotional power may be expressed outwardly or turned against oneself.

Ankh. *See* Crosses.

Antahkarana. The link between higher and lower minds, often called the "rainbow bridge." Containing three threads, the life thread (sutratma) and consciousness thread (also called antahkarana) are inherent; the creative thread is to be built in mental matter by the aspirant. Collectively these three threads become the antahkarana–the communication medium between the soul, the spiritual triad, and the lower mind of each individual.

Anthroposophy. Literally, "man-wisdom." RUDOLF STEINER's system of AGELESS WISDOM within the esoteric Christian tradition. Steiner began in the THEOSOPHICAL SOCIETY but established his own more Christian perspective closely resembling ROSICRUCIANS. His centers emphasize EURYTHMY, gardening, and community. WALDORF SCHOOLS have their origins in Steiner's teachings.

Apocalypse. Traditionally, revelation or disclosure of what will occur in the last days of the world. In the esoteric tradition, we think of this as the closing of an era, with its revelations and karmic lessons being satisfied.

Apport. An object or being materialized by spirit through the use of unknown laws of manifestation, often accompanying a seance or contact with a powerful nonphysical being.

Appropriate response. A phrase bequeathed by mystery teachings that acknowledges we must consider many factors, weigh them, and create a response that witnesses to inner, as well as outer, awareness. The conscious shaping of a response to produce the greatest possible good for all concerned. A response formed as a result of a thorough evaluation and guided by our highest intuitiion.

Aquarian Age. The period within the 26,000-year cycle called the "Great Year" in which Earth is subject to the influence of the constellation Aquarius, astronomically and astrologically. Each of twelve periods, or world ages, in a Great Year–each approximately 2500 years long–characterizes one of the twelve zodiacal signs. The planet Earth has completed the cycle, or world age, in which energies from the constellation Pisces dominated and has now moved into a new period, the Age of Aquarius. In the Aquarian Age, the emphasis is on inner and outer peace, cooperation, interdependence, and the global community.

Archangel (of the celestial hierarchy of a constellation). Considered to be one of the highest of the guiding influences which exist under each constellation to energize and influence planetary life. The archangels of a constellation bestow the blessings of that constellation upon the physical planet, the astral world, and upon humanity, according to regular cyclic intervals.

Archangels. The most advanced beings of the angelic kingdom who have risen above the limitations of individuality and entered into universal or cosmic consciousness, as have the adepts from the human kingdom. Highest among this group are the seven solar archangels, or the Seven Mighty Spirits before the Throne. A vast group of beings, the archangels act as the directors of the evolution of life and form in every dimension. The four best-known archangels guide humanity through the seasons of the year: Raphael (spring), Uriel (summer), Michael (autumn), and Gabriel (winter). Included in the guardians of the angelic ranks and initiations are the Cloud of Silent Watchers: the Seraphim, Cherubim, and Thrones–the highest angelic grouping. The next four advanced orders are the Dominions, Powers, Virtues, and Principalities. The concluding orders are the Archangels and the Angels.

The Four Mighty Archangels

Gabriel. Archangel of Winter Solstice is considered the guardian of mothers and the young of both the human and animal kingdoms. He is said to be the teacher of Mother Mary. His angelic assistants lead the celestial music at the time of the solstice and of CHRIST-MAS, we are told.

Raphael. Archangel of Spring Equinox and considered a major influence in the field of healing. Raphael is in charge of both lesser healing angels and the energies of rejuvenation.

Uriel. Archangel of Summer Solstice, Uriel is viewed as the one who paints faces in the clouds and colors the flowers. He brings the blessings of fulfillment.

Michael. Archangel of Fall Equinox and considered the fierce defender of justice and faith. Often seen as the one who reminds us to see what seeds we are planting and thus what we shall harvest in the long run. He is mentioned in the Christian tradition as the Principal Helper of the Christ.

Archetypal Logos. A great being supervising the divine Plan for a given group of solar systems. He holds the Plan while other Logoi bring it into manifestation at their levels of command.

Archetypal world. The great reservoir of archetypal energies held in abeyance from which are drawn creative ideas, energies, and forces on every level. In kabalistic thought, Atziluth.

Archetype. Greek from *arche*, meaning "old or basic," and *typos*, meaning "type or form." A pattern or blueprint held in the inner planes to guide and assist the lower planes in forming or evolving. The container of subtle energies, to be used in modeling oneself. Also used for basic symbols of consciousness, and as by CARL JUNG, belonging to a collective language of religion or myth. Preserves a more personal energy that can transform or act upon the nature of one who keys into them.

Archons. In Greek, "ruler." Invisible, godlike rulers of the world of appearances. Often depicted as a hierarchy; their leader is the DEMIURGE. Though they may be descended from the true God, they do not know him and try to keep the human seeker from reaching him. Often identified with the planets, they are sometimes given various names of the Old Testament God, e.g., Adonai, Sabaoth, etc.

Arhat. A wise one whose work now (having received the fourth INITIATION) is in preparation for the next level. Purification of the nature of human traits is primary, and pain a principal tool until will aligns to higher influences. This stage is to solar initiation as probationer is to first human initiation.

Arjuna. The initiate-being instructed by KRISHNA, as found in the BHAGAVAD GITA.

"As above, so below." The HERMETIC PRINCIPLE of Correspondence, one of seven postulates underlying the spiritual laws of creation.

Asana. A physical posture designated as significant for the stimulation of life energy in HATHA YOGA.

Ascendant (also known as rising sign). This constellation – located on the horizon at the time of birth, calculated according to birth date, time, and location–is of prime importance to the determination of the personal trinity. The sign on the eastern horizon or first house cusp in an individual's natal chart, or horoscope.

Ascension, the. The fifth step in the Christian Path of Initiation; in the life of Jesus, the Christ, when the body was lifted into higher vibrations and was no longer apparent from a physical perspective.

Ashram. A spiritual environment especially designed for the advancement of consciousness according to the needs of a particular practice.

"As if" technique. A conscious choice to work "as if" a desired reality already exists, instilling the affirmation that it will come to pass, while at the same time meeting the lessons to be learned as if it were already so.

Aspect. An angle formed by the placement or relationship between two or more planets in an astrological chart. The degree of the angle determines whether the relationship it describes is harmonious, inharmonious, or challenging.

Aspirant. One who consciously seeks acceptance upon the spiritual path. More specifically, a person on the PROBATIONARY PATH, the beginning stages of conscious spiritual growth.

Aspiration. The stimulation of high ideals or images for focusing and lifting devotion; use of deity to uplift human values.

Assagioli, Roberto. b. Venice, 1888, d. 1974. Young colleague of Freud and Jung in psychoanalytic studies who formulated a new concept in transpersonal psychology called "PSYCHOSYNTHESIS." He believed that, in addition to the individual, conscious self or "I," every person experiences spiritual realities to be used on the evolutionary pathway to higher consciousness. He founded the Institute of Psychosynthesis in 1926 and in 1932 began teaching with Alice Bailey at her school on Lake Maggiore, considered to be of the Agni Yoga tradition. Incarcerated by Fascists during World War II, he began life-long investigations into advanced techniques of meditation and altered states of consciousness, training many in tech-

niques of telepathy and clairvoyance. *Psychosynthesis: A Manual of Principles and Techniques,* 1965; *Act of Will,* 1973.

Assiah. The name given by Kabalah to the physical, material world of form; the outer field of human endeavors; the world of lowest vibration.

Astral. Literally translated "starry" for energy and "bursts" of activity that collect in this sensitive, feeling level of being.

Astral body. The emotional, or "starry," body easily imprinted by collective energies, as well as energies of others in our vicinity. This emotional disposition is by nature unstable and powerful. As it is cleared, the astral body serves as a battery of energy to assist the soul in fulfilling its purpose.

Astral dimension (also, world of illusion, or desire world). The nonmaterial astral world – consisting of the astral and lower mental planes – is subject to laws other than those operating in the physical world or in the higher worlds of mind and spirit. This reflected plane of being, of a different nature than the etheric dimension, flows through the physical world, interpenetrating chemical and etheric regions of the physical and influencing the activities of this sphere. Composed of what may be described as force-matter, this dimension is not a fine gradation of chemical matter but the sensitive ethers of life, feeling, and emotion. As they assume tangible form in this force-matter, feelings, sensations, and emotions each have a particular form, color, and rate of vibration. The combined emotional and lower mental states of humanity form a globe-encircling, globe-penetrating cloud, or aura, which constitutes a world of its own–the astral dimension. Its dominant laws are attraction, repulsion, metamorphosis, and transformation. This realm is inhabited by innumerable sensate beings who operate in diverse subtle ways to influence humanity through desires and emotions. Dominated by desires and living without physical forms, they are still capable of influencing others and growing themselves. A living record in feeling, picture, sound, and color of the happenings of all planet life is preserved in this world.

Astral light workers. Awakened ones who actively distribute light and love through their consciousness as a service to those in need. These invisible helpers may be in physical embodiment, or they may operate strictly from spiritual realms.

Astral plane. The reflective ethers that record the sensitive, feeling level of beings called the emotional nature of individuals. Also, the emotional dimension of the collective.

Astral senses. Senses which psychically perceive the less dense or more subtle frequencies, i.e., feelings or thoughts; these senses are to the feeling nature what physical senses are to dense bodies.

Astral travel. The experience of the separate dream-body, motivated by desire, that leaves behind the physical form to move about in the nonphysical reality behind the veil of sleep. Also called astral projection. *See* Out-of-body experience.

Astral vehicle. The astral body, less material than the physical body, is the emotional matter inter-penetrating the physical body.

Astrology. *See pages 14-17.*

Atomic plane (and sub-planes). The plane used by the MONAD to send forth its will toward denser reality to be expressed by the soul. Lowest level of monad and highest level of soul expression.

Astrology – a science and an art

The study of the influence on humanity and planetary life of the vibratory radiations of the Sun, the Moon, and other celestial bodies in their various positions and relationships. The practice of astrology is considered both an art and a science. The **astrology chart** (also known as horoscope) is a map or diagram of the heavens calculated to gain information regarding the impact and influence of the Sun, Moon, and planets upon specific people and/or events. A chart is constructed according to the exact date, time, and location of the event. *See* Celestial hierarchies.

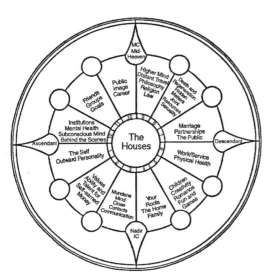

Astrological sun sign profiles. Great archetypes to help understand the influence to which they are attuned. Each person has three major influences active in the personality's makeup: sun, moon, and ascendant. These three create each personality with certain uniquenesses. However, sun sign influences are readily apparent.

Aries (approximately March 20 to April 20). Recognized strengths: youthfully vital, warm, bright, dynamic, independent, assertive, courageous; initiator and leader. Potential weaknesses: impatient, headstrong, arrogant, intrusive, lacks perseverance, quick to over-react. Element: fire. Hidden helper: Libra. Virtue: enthusiasm. Ruled by Mars. Motto: "I am."

Taurus (approx. April 20 to May 20). Recognized strengths: hard-working, stable, persistent, responsible, determined, patient, reliable, slow to anger; cherishes nature and loves to create beauty. Potential weaknesses: stubborn (as a bull), materialistic, sexual nature may dominate, slow, selfish. Element: earth. Hidden helper: Scorpio. Virtue: beauty. Ruled by Venus. Motto: "I have, I hold."

Gemini (approx. May 20 to June 20). Recognized strengths: quick-minded, versatile, alert, inventive, chatty, adaptable, sociable, energetic. Potential weaknesses: fickle, judgmental, easily scattered; over-commits. Element: air. Hidden helper: Sagittarius. Virtue: universality. Ruled by Mercury. Motto: "I think."

Cancer (approx. June 20 to July 20). Recognized strengths: nurturing, home-loving; supportive, patriotic, sensitive, tenacious; listens well. Potential weaknesses: possessive, over-reactive, evasive, emotional. Element: water. Hidden helper: Capricorn. Virtue: leadership. Ruled by Moon. Motto: "I feel."

Leo (approx. July 20 to Aug. 20). Recognized strengths: courageous, perceptive, generous, affectionate, creative, receptive, self-confident, seeks the limelight. Potential weaknesses: egocentric, selfish, domineering, proud, over-bearing. Element: fire. Hidden helper: Aquarius. Virtue: love. Ruled by Sun. Motto: "I will."

Virgo (approx. Aug. 20 to Sept. 20). Recognized strengths: detail-oriented, intelligent, discerning, self-disciplined, analytical, hard-working, unassuming; self-examiner. Potential weaknesses: judgmental, negative, critical, skeptical; low self-esteem. Element: earth. Hidden helper: Pisces. Virtue: purity. Ruled by Mercury. Motto: "I analyze."

Libra (approx. Sept. 20 to Oct. 20). Recognized strengths: perceptive, charming, sociable, diplomatic; negotiator, lover of harmony, justice, and beauty. Potential weaknesses: indecisive, codependent, quick to swing to opposite pole, unexpected rigidity. Element: air. Hidden helper: Aries. Virtue: reverence. Ruled by Venus. Motto: "I balance."

Scorpio (approx. Oct. 20 to Nov. 20). Recognized strengths: enduring, intense, sexually alluring, introspective, practical, never superficial; admirable recuperative powers. Potential weaknesses: secretive, vindictive, purposefully mysterious, sexually excessive, lacking in self-understanding. Element: water. Hidden helper: Taurus. Virtue: transformation. Ruled by Pluto. Motto: "I desire."

 Sagittarius (approx. Nov. 20 to Dec. 20). Recognized strengths: quick-witted, analytical, philosophical, straightforward, friendly, optimistic, honest, independent, fun, enthusiastic, direct; loves travel and freedom. Potential weaknesses: fickle, sharp-tongued or blunt, truthful to a fault; can be shattered. Element: fire. Hidden helper: Gemini. Virtue: harmlessness. Ruled by Jupiter. Motto: "I perceive."

Capricorn (approx. Dec. 20 to Jan. 20). Recognized strengths: stable, progresses slowly, goal-oriented, obedient to rules and regulations, achieving, self-disciplined, reliable, persevering. Potential weaknesses: materialistic, fearful, conservative, excessively ambitious, overly cautious; needs recognition, may be melancholy. Element: earth. Hidden helper: Cancer. Virtue: fearlessness. Ruled by Saturn. Motto: "I see."

Aquarius (approx. Jan. 20 to Feb. 20). Recognized strengths: generous, inventive, detached, progressive, tolerant, ingenuous, open-minded, social, creative; problem-solver, humanitarian. Potential weaknesses: unconventional, eccentric, changeable, independent to a fault, unsteady, aloof. Element: air. Hidden helper: Leo. Virtue: humility. Ruled by Uranus. Motto: "I know."

Pisces (approx. Feb. 20 to March 20). Recognized strengths: imaginative, sensitive, spiritual, sympathetic, compassionate, charming, dramatic, humorous, impressionable, kind, gentle, graceful. Potential weaknesses: depressive, addictive, evasive; low vitality, may lack will power. Element: water. Hidden helper: Virgo. Virtue: joy. Ruled by Neptune. Motto: "I believe."

At-one-ment. A state of unity with the One Source of which humanity is capable, whereby the many parts of creation can become whole.

Attached entity. *See* Spirit attachment.

Attachment. A barrier to illumination due to the conscious or unconscious refusal to forgive or release the distortions held.

Attunement. A technique for becoming one in vibration with. The natural state of blending with our surroundings.

 Atziluth. In Kabalah, the fiery world of spirit, the home of archetypal energy of creation.

Aum. *See* Om.

Aura. A subtle emanation of the energy pattern of a soul, composed of the physical body, the emotional nature, the mental make-up, and the soul in its field of activity.

Aurobindo, Sri Ghose. b. Calcutta, 1872, d. 1950. Philosopher, mystic, educator, and poet. The guiding force behind a spiritual community at Pondicherry, French India, called Auroville Ashram, whose purpose was to bring about the salvation of society by the individual attainment of higher consciousness. He and his disciple, MIRA RICHARDS, known as "The Mother," delivered a set of

17

teachings to the world called Integral Yoga. *The Life Divine,* 1940; *The Synthesis of Yoga,* 1948; *Aurobindo on Himself,* 1953.

Avalokita. Sanskrit for "the Lord who is perceived or cognized"; the spiritual entity whose influence is perceived and felt; the Soul unfolded and expressing, as in ADEPT or MASTER.

Avatar. An incarnation of God; the descent of Divinity into human form. One who is not bound by the wheel of rebirth and comes to humanity as a messenger from the world of spirit in order to bless and aid humanity in its spiritual growth. The divine potency embodied in an avatar acts as a regenerative power for humankind and appears approximately once each age, usually near the beginning of a new era.

Avatar of Synthesis. An Agni term. The expected one who will be the guiding consciousness of the new era. Little can be said of this Great Mystery except that the consciousness of this forthcoming Avatar will overlight and reinforce the work of the Christ. The Avatar will only influence us through the mental plane, promoting good will, harmony, unity, seeking to do away with separativeness.

Awakened ones. Those aware of deity and desirous of interacting with higher realities.

Awakening, the. Secondary influence of human nature that stirs and becomes conscious of a path to high consciousness (the primary influence being survival).

B

Babaji. A name given to many Hindu saints meaning "dear father" or "holy father."

Babaji Herakhan. A saint who reincarnates in the northern Himalayas, appearing and disappearing at will, and said to create a body without birth, merely calling his form into manifestation as needed. He said, "I shall never leave my physical body. It will always remain visible to at least a small number of people on this earth." He specifically incarnated in 1970 through 1984 when he took MAHASAMADHI, returning to spirit, and is considered the supreme guru of the Self-Realization Fellowship. Babaji's disciple, Lahiri Mahasaya, received the KRIYA YOGA from him to pass on as a means to "control sensory mind and intellect; and to banish desire, fear, and anger." Kriya Yoga is cited twice in the *Bhagavad Gita.* Paramahansa Yogananda, *Autobiography of a Yogi,* 1946.

Bailey, Alice A. b. Manchester, England, 1880, d. 1949. Theosophist and spiritualist writer. She was first visited in 1919 by MASTER DJWHAL KHUL, spiritual guide also called "the Tibetan," who dictated the ancient wisdom teachings to her over a 30-year period. These comprise twenty volumes known as the Bailey books. In 1923, she founded the Arcane School in New York, seeking to establish a worldwide organization unifying traditions of East and West. *Light from the Soul,* 1927; *The Great Invocation,* 1937; *The Reappearance of the Christ,* 1948.

Ballard, Guy Warren. b. Kansas, 1878, d. 1939. Founder of the "I AM" religious activity, an offshoot of ROSICRUCIANISM. He claimed to have been visited by Comte de Saint GERMAIN, the ascended MASTER, who had come to initiate the Seventh Golden Age of Eternal Perfection on Earth and to disseminate teachings on the Great Law of Life. With his wife, Edna Anne Ballard, he established the Saint Germain Press and the Saint Germain Foundation, giving rise to a number of like-minded groups and much channeled material. *Unveiled Mysteries,* 1934; *The Magic Presence,* 1935; *The "I AM" Discourses,* 1936.

Ball of knowledge. The understanding and awareness gathered through many experiences (other lives) and retained by the high self—data which can be brought to consciousness.

Baptism. A ritual invoking spiritual forces and guardians to assist us when encountering the challenges of physical life. This sacrament strengthens the sheath of spiritual energy about us, calling for a guardian from spirit and from the human side. Both guardians have a spiritual relationship to that one whom they serve. The rite opens the aura to environmental influence. Parents and godparents commit themselves to assisting soul in conscious growth. In baptism, the aura (our protective covering) is ruptured, invoking grace to consciously foster spiritual growth.

Bardo. The after-life reality through which we travel as we process our life review, confronting emotional situations and unfinished business to see if we have sufficiently released seeds of KARMA to be freed from their influence.

Basic self (also, basic nature, lower self, or self). The personality we choose to come into this life, possessing certain characteristics, such as masculine and feminine traits. These unique qualities modify the physical, emotional, and mental natures to form the personality. More than the subconscious nature, it includes our specific emotional and mental patterns, intuitive capacities, likes and dislikes, etc.

Beacon of achievement. An Agni term. One who stands purified and radiant with the manifestation of cosmic fire. "Few understand how the dwellers themselves can be like beacons." *(Fiery World,* 1615) Thus Agni yogis contain within their centers the cosmic fire that transforms them into beacons.

Beauty. Agni virtue for Taurus. Beauty is sustenance to the emerging spirit. It bestows the ability to see and apprehend splendor in the world. Knowing beauty is in the eye of the beholder, we usually see first the beauty of things, then nature, then we come to behold the light in another. As we do so, we learn to be the beauty that is needed to illumine the world.

Besant, Annie Wood. b. London, 1847, d. 1933. Theosophist, feminist, and president of the Indian National Congress in 1919. She is noted for her stand in favor of birth control in such an unlikely era as the 1870s and founding the Freethought Publishing Company with Charles Bradlaugh. A devoted student of Madame Blavatsky's ancient wisdom teachings and investigations into the occult, she collaborated with Charles Leadbeater on *Man: Whence, How and Whither,* 1913, an examination of human history as an evolutionary journey. *The Ancient Wisdom*, 1897; *Esoteric Christianity*, 1901; *The Spiritual Life*, 1912.

Bhagavad Gita. The Hindu sacred writings; a part of the great Hindu epic *Mahabharata*. A teaching segment is excerpted as a sacred text, translated into English as *The Song of God.*

Bhakti Yoga. *See* Yoga.

Binah. The third sephirah on the kabalistic TREE OF LIFE and the highest sephirah on the feminine pillar; also called the "Superior Mother."

Biorhythm. A system of measuring and plotting the flow of energy in the physical, emotional, and mental dimensions of our nature.

Black magic. The art of selfish use of power to enhance ego or materialism or to manipulate others. *Magick* as an old term meant "transformation or transformational powers." Thus, the misuse of spiritual powers for the gratification of the ego.

Blavatsky, Helena Petrovna. b. the Ukraine, 1831, d. 1891. Widely acclaimed occultist, psychic, and adept who in 1875, with Henry Steel Olcott, founded the THEOSOPHICAL SOCIETY to "promote universal brotherhood, study various religions of the world, and investigate psychic phenomena." *The Secret Doctrine*–cited as the "authentic sourcebook" for the birth, structure, and evolution of the universes, solar systems, and our Earth's humanities–is considered her great work. She was a disciple of MASTER MORYA and imparted his teachings as Theosophy, formalizing concepts of REINCARNATION and KARMA, spiritual hierarchy, and the Divine Plan. She taught that theosophy was "divine ethics" and that the way must be prepared for the coming of the LORD MAITREYA who would issue in a new cycle in human evolution. *Isis Unveiled*, 1877; *The Secret Doctrine, The Key to Theosophy, The Voice of Silence*, all published 1889.

Blended heart. An Agni term. A clue to a prerequisite for spiritual advancement–the integration of thinking and feeling. A blended heart is able to perceive, empathize, understand, and adjust to demands consistent to unfolding spiritual maturity.

Blood of the heart. This symbol of outer life stands for personality desires; it represents the grief and suffering through which the heart frees itself of desire domination.

Blue Moon. In astrology, a **second** full Moon in any given Sun sign period, each of which is approximately thirty days–an infrequent occurrence at irregular intervals.

Bodhisattva. Sanskrit for one who carries buddhic energy and in a future incarnation will become a BUDDHA (enlightened to NIRVANA), or one whose consciousness has become enlightened intelligence, or BUDDHI. Used much like West-

ern spiritual traditions use "Christed." In the East the office presently occupied by the LORD MAITREYA, known in the occident as the Christ. This office is that of world teacher, head of all religions of the world, Master of Masters, and teacher of angels and of humanity. A Bodhisattva is the exponent of Ray 2 force.

Bodhisattva of Compassion. The oriental title given most frequently to the personification of the DIVINE FEMININE. "KUAN YIN," in the way Queen of Peace refers to Holy Mary, Mother of Jesus. The masculine version of the Bodhisattva of Compassion is named Avalokiteshvara and translates "one who looks down from on high."

Boehme, Jakob. b. Germany, 1575, d. 1624. A simple Medieval cobbler of peasant stock who became a revered Christian mystic. As a youth, he discovered the ability to enter abnormal states of consciousness and see into the astral light. Though apprenticed as a shoemaker, he was able to read and write and, in 1612, recounted the visions he had experienced from boyhood. As foretold by a stranger under mysterious circumstances, he was maligned and persecuted throughout his life. Boehme advocated an esoteric, cosmic understanding of Christ and maintained his writings described only what he had learned from Divine Illumination; that no one needed assistance from the established church to find fulfillment in Christ. He believed that God reconciles all opposites, is the basis of all being, and the source of all energy; that existing things are the signature of God. *The Signature of All Things*, 1621; *Mysterium Magnum*, 1623; *The Way to Christ*, 1623.

"Born again." The spiritual birth which occurs in the physical world, or secular reality. The spiritual empowerment of "babes in Christ," candidates for the teachings to whom spiritual reality extends–"eyes with which to see and ears with which to hear." The second (nonphysical) birth–as the "birth of the Christ-within"–and the third can be realized by initiates of a disciplined nature, when we proceed to soul maturity.

Brahma, also Brahman. In Hinduism, the essential divine reality of the universe; the eternal spirit from which all being originates and to which all return.

Brahmin. In Hinduism, a member of the highest caste–originally made up of priests, now of a more diverse group.

Briah. One of the four worlds of the Kabalah, Briah is the World of Creation, also called Khorsis, or the World of Thrones. Here, the sephiroth which constitute the kabalistic TREE OF LIFE are manifest through the ten archangels. The sephiroth are regarded as emanations of deity and represent a group of exalted ideas, titles, and attributes, and a hierarchy of spiritual beings outside of humanity.

Brotherhood (the). The Hierarchy of ELDER BROTHERS BEFORE THE THRONE, as called in Christian tradition; saints and holy ones who have emerged from the human condition into greater oneness with the Christ. Having passed certain tests at first initiation, the aspirant is deemed worthy of the attention of the Brotherhood (or Hierarchy). Also known as the White Brotherhood or the Great White Brotherhood.

Brotherhood, dark. A formation of strong egos that seeks to restrict human evolution, tempting humans to emanate their love of power rather than to open the heart and learn love and service. These influences strengthen the forces of duality and individuality, catering to those in search of personal power and will, rather than yielding to higher will.

Brotherhood, White (or White Lodge). The Hierarchy of elders leading humanity in evolution. The term "white" is used as in "white magic" or positive transformation versus the path of darkness–the enhancing of ego.

Buddha. "The enlightened," a title bestowed upon one who has developed the buddhic principle of spiritual discrimination. Improperly used as a personal name, it is a title, as is "the Christ."

Buddha, Gautama Siddhartha. c. 563 B.C. "The Enlightened," who taught that the true self is God and God is the true self. His most important revelations concern the causes of suffering and the way in which salvation from suffering may be achieved. He experienced twenty-four lives while on the path as a bodhisattva, choosing to remain in the world to teach. The next bodhisattva to achieve buddhahood will be MAITREYA.

Buddha consciousness. Correlates in Eastern thought to Christ consciousness, meaning an enlightened state of consciousness, or lifted into holy awareness.

Buddhi. The love of the spiritualized heart, spiritual wisdom, or compassion useful in softening the destructive mind. Often refers to the energy of heart and mind blended and balanced.

Buddhic level (or plane). The intuitive, spiritual or CHRIST CONSCIOUSNESS level of expression that is the door to COSMIC CONSCIOUSNESS. Ideas stream from this intuitional plane in a manner comparable to the outpouring of the Holy Spirit in traditional Christian terms. A spiritual level of mind that perceives higher will, intelligence, and love and is able to vibrate these energies to the maturing soul.

Buddhism. A world religion with four major branches, Buddhism has grown from the teachings of Guatama Siddhartha, who lived about 500 years prior to Christ. Siddhartha became the Buddha and anchored the wisdom principle, just as Jesus became the Christ and anchored the love principle.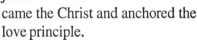

Building the cup. The gradual creation within the human mental body of a receiver/container for the droplets of wisdom that come from the CLOUD OF KNOWABLE THINGS usually during meditation, when teaching or inspired. The cup makes it possible to retain and record inspiration so that it doesn't merely dissipate without being anchored or noted.

Byzantine Empire. A.D. 395-1453 in Southeast Europe and Southwest Asia. The Byzantine Christian tradition helps the modern Christian world relate to Eastern traditions, bridging older Christian teachings, the esoteric, and those of the early church. In A.D. 1054, the church divided into the Roman church and the Church of Constantinople, now known as the Eastern or Byzantine branch.

C

Campbell, Joseph. b. New York City, 1904, d. 1987. Educator, author, and foremost authority on the mythologies of the world. It was said that he knew "the vast sweep of man's panoramic past as few men have ever known it." His profound knowledge and extensive scholarship revealed current themes from the sacred scriptures and mythologies of the world's broadly divergent races and cultures, which he believed (as did Carl Jung) to be the master keys to the human psyche, "capable of bridging the past and future and the worlds of East and West." *The Masks of God,* Vols. I-IV, 1959-1967; *Myths, Dreams and Religions,* 1970; *Myths to Live By,* 1972.

Carryovers. Negative memories held as sensations and feelings that need to be dissolved and replaced by pure or positive energy.

Catholic. Latin for "universal, all-inclusive."

Causal body. An out-of-date term for the level of Buddhic/Christ consciousness, the point from which the soul projects itself into the sheaths of the lower world–mental, emotional, and physical. The cause behind personality.

Cause and Effect (Hermetic principle of). Known also as the law of KARMA: every thought, every belief, every action has a reaction, an effect. Noted in the Christian tradition as "casting one's bread upon the water" to return in due time in the wisdom of the Higher; also as the concept that we shall reap what we have sown. *See* Ecclesiastes 11.1 and Galatians 6.7-9, respectively.

Cayce, Edgar. b. Kentucky, 1877, d. 1945. The clairvoyant and psychic diagnostician, known as "The Sleeping Prophet," was of humble birth and limited education. His inexplicably accurate readings astonished contemporary physicians: while in a self-induced trance state, he was able to identify specific health problems and their remedy; he often provided information on previous incarnations. His work is commemorated by the Association for Research and Enlightenment, Virginia Beach, Virginia. Biography by Thomas Sugrue: *There Is a River,* 1942; *Auras,* 1945; *What I Believe,* 1946; *Edgar Cayce on Atlantis,* 1968.

Celestial Hierarchies. *See pages 29-32.*

Celibacy. The practice of sexual self-discipline by nonparticipation. In the best sense of the word, celibacy is raising the spiritual forces spent in sexual expression to another level of creativity. The primary function of celibacy is to help the practitioner break the instinctual gratification of the sexual self and learn to relate on a higher level. *See* Periodic abstinence.

Cellular memory. The imprint of life contained in even the smallest atom that retains our record of experience, usually unconscious or instinctual.

Celts. The ancient indigenous people of Western Europe whose religion was matriarchal and nature-based. Often referred to today as DRUIDS, the title given their scholars. They worshiped outdoors, often in groves; the tree and mistletoe were their sacred symbols. The Druids were chiefs, scholars, judges, and magicians, forming the basis of most European shamanistic religions.

Centered and balanced. Implies a state of equilibrium or harmony between spirit and matter, inspiration and expression.

Centering. A technique to harmonize our lower nature, making it sensitive to the presence of the nonphysical nature.

Chakra. Literally, "wheel." A Sanskrit term designating energy centers, actual vortices of force latent within the etheric body of every human: crown, brow (AJNA), throat, heart, solar plexus, abdomen, root. Corresponding to different levels of consciousness and controlling the physical condition of the area of the body which they influence, the centers activate as we awaken to nonphysical reality and as we become increasingly aware of higher vibrations and extended realities.

Celestial Hierarchies

A group of intelligences responsible for the framework of the cosmos and for transmitting the qualities of the Triune God to humanity. A series of graded beings, comprising three triads which, in descending order, are: 1) Seraphim, Cherubim, Thrones; 2) Dominions, Virtues, Powers; 3) Principles, Archangels, and Angels. These beings represent and are sustained by the divine Source and are most often referred to as angels, from a Greek word meaning "one who acts as messenger from the celestial realms to the world of humankind." Within this structure twelve zodiacal hierarchies are charged with cosmic creative energies and project specific archetypal ideas and influences into the universe which then are registered in human consciousness and translated into action according to each person's evolutionary status. A person living consciously uses these energies to enhance life and grow spiritually. The specific celestial hierarchies are:

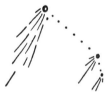 The name of the hierarchical rulers of the **constellation of Aries** is not given, though this celestial hierarchy is related to the **Lords of Fire.** The vibration of this powerful group–said to hold the archetype of the new Christed human being who will be increasingly manifested in the coming era–is considered to be too high to be relayed to humanity at this time.

The rulers of the **constellation of Taurus** work under a hierarchy whose name is unrevealed. They teach form-building through the use of sound, or the Word, to vibrate and to create. This holy, unnamed order steps divine will toward Earth through the **Lords of Karma** (also known as the LIPIKAS) 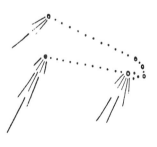 who impress each soul with its purpose for incarnation. Parallel to the THRONES of the angelic kingdom, these Lords assist in bringing about divine justice through the universal law of cause and effect, reminding us that "as we sow, so shall we reap." Currently humanity is satisfying much of the KARMA of the past in preparation for the new era.

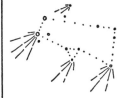

The **Lords of Mercury,** also known as the SERAPHIM, whose power and grandeur surpass all description, guide humanity toward initiatory work. These fiery, enthusiastic beings are among the most advanced of the angelic kingdom and a part of the CLOUD OF SILENT WATCHERS. The word *seraphim* comes from the Hebrew word *seraph,* meaning "love." The third aspect of the holy trinity, the Holy Spirit–deliverer of gifts of the spirit–influences meditations during the reign of the **constellation of Gemini,** often bringing profound revelations.

These hierarchical rulers of the **constellation of Cancer,** the CHERUBIM, are among the most advanced of the angelic kingdom and a part of the Cloud of Silent Watchers. Their most important work is to protect sacred places. Coworking with Capricorn and the Archangels, these forces, often called the "waters of life," blend the mystical energies of spirit and matter.

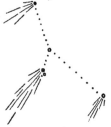

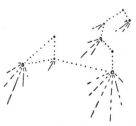

The Lords of Flame (or Love), one of the great hierarchies of spiritual beings who guides the solar system, rule the **constellation of Leo.** These exalted beings of love, light, and spiritual power inspire humanity in its journey to higher consciousness, to self-mastery. With their assistance we can comprehend our inherent capability to demonstrate these attributes responsibly in our lives. They are said to have taken control of the evolution of humanity 18 million years ago, during the middle of the Lemurian, or third, ROOT RACE.

The hierarchical rulers of the **constellation of Virgo,** the **Lords of Wisdom,** hold the power by which life ensouls form. They enter into perfect attunement so that mind and matter can become as one. The cosmic madonna, symbol of Virgo, sacrifices (makes sacred) herself to nurture and sustain life on the planet as a place for these souls to incarnate.

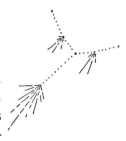

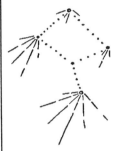

The hierarchical rulers of the **constellation of Libra** teach humanity to translate assertiveness into cooperation. These **Lords of Individuality** help us learn to live the ideal of the greatest good for the greatest number while also appreciating our unique gifts, value, and capabilities.

The **Lords of Form,** hierarchical rulers of the **constellation of Scorpio,** have created patterns of cosmic thoughtforms for humanity that hold profound energy for change, rejuvenation, and revitalization–the key elements for healing and renewal.

The hierarchical rulers of the **constellation of Sagittarius, the Lords of Mind,** are waiting until humans develop enough to be able to use wisely the power of divine mind. These arcing, dancing, mental powers stimulate intellect and invention. Higher human initiates capable of responding to this hierarchy are cutting the path for us all; as these trailblazers discover and anchor the potentials, all of humanity benefits.

Here in the **constellation of Capricorn** we most often relate to initiation, tests, and anchoring changes into the physical plane. The **archangels** are the guardians of rank and initiation, each holding a pattern humanity must assimilate. Gradually the initiate passes the tests and acquires the many facets needed to become the MASTER.

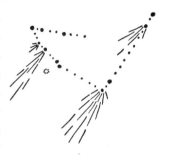

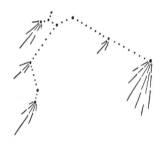

The constellation of Aquarius is the home of the celestial hierarchy of the **angels** and of those who pass from Earth in infancy, until time for the next life arrives. Many disciples are guided by angelic forces without outer awareness, while others work consciously with light beings under the tutelage of this hierarchy. The energy of the Aquarian Age encourages right-relationship between humanity and the angelic kingdom. We have much to learn about etheric reality from them–certainly in one of their most important areas, healing.

The celestial hierarchy of the **constellation of Pisces** is known as the **Lords of Compassion.** Having learned the power of unconditional love, these advanced ones in whom BUDDHI of the heart is activated hold 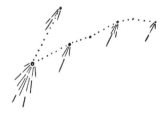 the human kingdom in a balance of love and wisdom to stimulate unconditional love within the group mind. Bequeathing light and love impartially, they nurture humanity in its painful condition, loving the imperfect and the ignorant without shirking and leading the human kingdom toward super-human evolution, also called the KINGDOM OF SOULS.

Chalice. Symbolically, the receptive mind seeking spiritual growth, guidance, and blessing. The open high consciousness that can receive inspiration, vision, and direct knowledge from the Christ; the form built in order to contact and receive the energies of the spiritual triad. The monadic, or divine, current flowing to lower levels of consciousness creates a whirlpool of energy on the higher mental plane. This vortex resembles a cup formed of nine flower-like petals–the chalice or the lotus in esoteric literature, enclosing three pearls. Later, in this center will emerge the jewel, or spark of fire, of the MONAD–the real Self. In the chalice is anchored the eternal guide, the SOLAR ANGEL, who leads the individual spark of divine life to awareness of the true SELF through the process of awakening and initiations. The human soul communicates through the chalice with the worlds of density: physical, emotional, and mental realities. Also known as the LOTUS and the Temple of Solomon.

Channel. A particular state of consciousness in which energy can flow from level to level. Channeling is a technique in which a person serves to bring information or influence from one dimension to another. Often called "trance mediums" in the past. Channeling lends itself to glamour and abuse.

Chanting. Repetitive vocalizing–spoken or sung–designed to penetrate the subconscious to affect the life of an aspirant.

Chaos. An Agni term. When used 🔥 without capitalization, "chaos" simply means disorder and confusion, the customary term; however, when capitalized, "Chaos" refers to the primordial substance of creation, the prima materia of the alchemists, the first outpouring, in theosophical terms. Chaos may be interpreted as the third aspect of the trinity, personified as the eternal feminine, the divine mother, the Goddess–superior to all feminine influences and corresponding to BINAH in KABALAH.

Chaos, the law of. The manifestation of a breaking down or return into the elements of creation; utter confusion. We live in a time of rediscovering certain "laws" of operation that apply at times of dissolution. These laws presently are being defined by physics, as well as metaphysicians and quantum physicists, as the "laws of chaos."

Chapels of Silence. A disciple is admitted at this initial point of specialized training behind the veil of sleep after some advancement has

33

been gained. Here we are exposed to currents, archetypal energies, and other stimuli to awaken inner forces, thus assisting those deemed ready to advance more rapidly in their tests and inner knowledge.

Chela. The dedicated student of a GURU; literally, a servant, i.e., handmaiden or servant of the Lord.

Cherubim. These angels supervise the elementals, emanate wisdom, intone truth, perceive the will, and hold the form for the Plan. These great beings are responsible for the form side of nature and for the motherhood of all life–a feminine, nurturing influence upon evolving life forms. As the celestial hierarchy of the constellation Cancer, they express clear truth and enlighten humanity with the energies of love and wisdom.

Chesed. The fourth sephirah on the TREE OF LIFE of the KABALAH, designated as Mercy and considered the home of the MASTERS. The teachings are that we cannot comprehend mercy until we have experienced severity. When we have integrated the lessons of severity and can now comprehend love in its many modes and phases – including tough love–we can then grant mercy for we have learned the purpose of discipline. Mercy can appropriately bequeath justice.

Chi. The Chinese word for "universal life energy." Sometimes "breath," as in "breath of life."

Child-like. The ability to experience the innocent basic nature of enthusiasm, spontaneity, trust, and openness, as do undamaged children filled with awe and wonder at the mystery of life. Freedom and joy abound without false limitations in the child-like state.

Child-within. The basic nature that retains childlike, enthusiastic, fresh, energetic qualities often hidden under programming, fears, false ideas, or distortions from previous experiences. To be thought of as the forever-young child part that can be set free to experience the events of life with freshness. Much healing can be accomplished on this level, so often distorted and wounded. Psychological efforts to heal this basic level of self aid in health maintenance and improvements, trust, the ability to mature in consciousness, and increased joy in living. *See* Inner child.

Chohan. A Lord, MASTER, or chief; a high ADEPT who has taken initiations beyond the five major initiations of the human kingdom, making him or her a "Master of Wisdom." High adepts who serve as the heads of the RAYS, such as MASTERS MORYA and KUTHUMI.

34

Chokmah. The second sephirah on the TREE OF LIFE of the Kabalah, known as Wisdom and masculine in nature on the pillar of "force."

Christ consciousness. A term the Christian tradition has used for intuitive knowing or the realization or attainment of high consciousness. The pure level of consciousness in which the mind, love, and will of God are made known to the enlightened person.

Christ Light. The illumination of God that emanates from and is experienced when we perceive and receive the energies of the divine Source. *See* Christ-within.

Christ, the. Head of HIERARCHY, teacher of angels and of humanity. The primary position of power for planet Earth, this living flame guides all life in this sphere of evolution.

Christ, the Cosmic. The second aspect of the Triune Godhead, also known as the Word or the Son, associated with love-wisdom. The divine creative center of the Supreme Being that disseminates the love and light of God. God creates and Christ formulates, while the Holy Spirit activates form. Every particle of physical life or energy comes from the visible Sun, while all spiritual energy comes from the invisible Sun or the Central Spiri-

tual Sun, also known as the Cosmic Christ. *See* Sun behind the Sun.

Christ, the historical. MASTER JESUS, the WAYSHOWER of the Christian Path of Discipleship. Each major event in his life correlates with a step along the Initiatory Path. Master Jesus built a pure form which was given to serve the Christ at the baptism. The title of "the Christ" was given to the high initiate, Jesus, as he served the Christ (planetary) in this unique way.

Christ, the mystical. Refers to the love aspect of the unfolding divine spirit within humanity. It is the divine life of the LOGOS which forms the garment of the Soul in each person, that humanity may know eternal life. The Christ principle that resides in every human heart; the Christ to be formed in each of us. This Immanent Spirit is born again and again in the heart and can never die but continues to develop throughout evolution until it is fully expressed in each human life. Also known as the Christ-within.

Christ, the planetary. The Archangel Christ who descended from the spiritual sheath of the Sun into the body of Master Jesus at the Baptism. The Lord Christ took upon himself the mission of transmuting the astral envelope of the Earth so purified substance would be available for humanity to build its astral bodies. The Christ incarnated in the body of Master Jesus; after the crucifixion, it withdrew into the Earth to become the indwelling planetary spirit. The planetary Christ functions as a SOLAR ANGEL for planetary life, guiding and guarding all kingdoms.

Christhood (or Buddhahood). The state of consciousness that aligns us with the Hierarchy of Earth, led by the Christ and realized by holy ones after the path of human initiation is completed.

Christian initiation. A process within Esoteric Christianity describing stages of growth; these five major steps are birth, baptism, transfiguration, crucifixion-resurrection, and ascension.

Christianity. The world religion that emerged out of the life and teachings of Jesus, the historical Christ. Gradually became formalized, utilizing the teachings as given to the world by his apostles.

Christmas. The celebration of the birth of Jesus, the initiate, celebrated at WINTER SOLSTICE until formally set at December 25. The principal festival of the water mysteries and the "festival of lights" for Christianity.

Christos. In Greek, "anointed." The anointed consciousness experienced a state of holy wisdom.

Christ-within. Also known as the Mystical Christ, the Christ Immanent, Inner Christ, HOPE OF GLORY. The divine nature incarnate within a human being; a spark or seed of the divine potential brought into increasing conscious awareness through attunement to the guiding consciousness of humanity, the planetary Christ, the Master of Masters, and teacher of angels and of humanity. We learn to unfold the Christ-within by practicing that presence in daily life. Illumination that emanates from and is experienced by those who perceive and receive energies of the divine Source. The love-wisdom aspect of the unfolding divine spirit within humanity that forms the garment of the soul in each person. The Christ principle resides in every human heart as a potential seed–to flower in each of us. This immanent spirit can never die but continues to develop throughout evolution until each human life fully expresses it.

Chrysalis. Symbolically, the unfolding soul encased in human form. Literally, a stage in the development of a butterfly in which the evolving life form is enclosed in a cocoon.

Churches of the Aquarian era. More akin to the early church than the organized church of the Middle Ages. This is in keeping with the challenging ideas of initiation–that greater power is gained at each step. The order of the initiation process: struggle to gain capability; calling for the test; taking the test itself; passing the test; transfer of energy, title, or recognition; then instability while learning to function in the new position.

apostolic: Participating in spiritual lineage all the way back to the Christ. Lineage established by the transformational gifts awakening. Enlightenment is the evidence.

catholic: Truly universal in nature, knowing in Christ all are one.

evangelical: Sharing the spirit; witnessing to the world through living ethical lives.

reformed: Renewed, reworked, made new and different by the ability to accept and adjust to the new incoming energies of the era.

Circle. Representing eternity, without beginning or end, the circle or ring signifies perfection, continuity, and completeness. The OUROBORUS is the FEATHERED SERPENT of the Western way, as the circle of creation enclosing the world soul.

Clairaudience. Clear-hearing–the facility of spiritual hearing that can hear psychically without limitation of matter, time, and space. Related to the throat center.

Clairsentience. Clear-feeling–the facility of spiritual feeling and sensing, without limitation of matter, time, and space. Related to the solar plexus center.

Clairvoyance. Clear-seeing–the facility of the spiritual eye that can see psychically, without limitations of matter, time, and space.

Cloud of Knowable Things. Thoughtforms contacted on higher levels of the mental plane from which can be drawn great beauty, wisdom, and inspiration; partly created by reflections of advanced thinkers who may be contacted telepathically. Also, the vast storehouse of knowledge into which flows the mind, love, and will of God from which the aspirant can receive inspiration through the awakening perceptions of high consciousness, thus finding that which we need for our ongoing pattern or evolution. Also known as the DHARMA LIGHT.

Cloud of Silent Watchers. Holy ones who care for humanity from higher planes. Often a reference to the archangels; similar to Elder

Brothers of Humanity. *See* Watcher.

Codependency. This modern term describes a personality too dependent upon others' responses–inner or outer–to shape his or her self-evaluation, self-esteem, and actions. Generally, codependency is developed between two needy people, neither of whom has healthy personal boundaries or a strong center; therefore, each is defined by the other's expectations. The single person suffering dependency seeks another equally needy to help define or reinforce lifestyle choices due to the lack of inner conviction.

Collective unconscious. Sum total of all levels of mind existing below the threshold of conscious awareness for all of humanity.

Collins, Mabel. Mrs. Keningale Cook, 19th century theosophist and writer of a series books of occult rules on self-knowledge and self-mastery published by the Theosophical Society. She said she received her prolific writings from the "Inner World." *Light on the Path* and *Through the Gates of Gold*, 1887; *When the Sun Moves Northward: The Way of Initiation*, 1923.

Color therapy. The use of color for its corrective influences on the physical, emotional, and/or mental body.

Comeasurement. An Agni term. The appropriate combination of energies through which purpose is achieved. A beautiful definition is given by Meditation Mount of Ojai, California: "Understanding that which is great and that which is small; what is distant and what is near; what we can attain and that which we would be fools to attempt...comeasurement is a true sense of proportion." Consideration of factors to be brought into right-relationship to achieve positive results.

Commandments. Rules established for practitioners of particular spiritual paths.

Common good. An Agni Yoga term for that which facilitates the evolution of the human family.

Communion, Holy, or Eucharist. In this Christian rite we experience the Lord's supper, the sacred meal of those committed to oneness with the Lord Christ in their inner world and oneness to each other. The celebrant stands as the representative of Christ, blessing the bread, wine, and water. Words of power are spoken, and accordingly the substance is changed. The full power of the ritual is disputed by denominations of the Christian faith, but esotericists believe this is the science of sacred contact, and the transubstantiation will be to the degree allowed by the receiver.

Community. A group of people united by a particular keynote or effort, joining consciousnesses of similar vibration for the purpose of being one in orientation. Each supports the others, and all acknowledge the oneness of their reason for being. Relationship is established by the realization of the similar inner nature and by the commitment to support that essence in each other as they mature.

Also, as an Agni theme: the family is the prototype of communal life personifying cooperation, the Hierarchy, and all conditions of brotherhood and sisterhood, but such families are rare. Community is creating family, a spiritual family, around the understanding we call like-mindedness or shared values. The ties are not just on the physical plane but extend into subtler levels as well. The Hierarchy of Chohans

is called "the community" in Agni Yoga. Community is the bonding of individuals in response to a keynote. Correlates to the energy and influence of the number 7.

Compassion. A blend of love and wisdom, the realization of "thinketh in the heart," sometimes considered a form of unconditional love.

Compassion, Bodhisattva of. A title given KUAN YIN, the personification of the Eastern divine feminine.

Competitive thinking. Smart, rational. I versus you.

Concentration. The power of focus; the ability to focus by will in such a way that we can burn through confusion and distraction to reach a centered point.

Concrete mind. This aspect of mind deals with concrete reality–tangible objects, knowable facts, measurable qualities. A lower level of mind with reference to abstract mind; the mid sub-plane(s) of the mental plane.

Confession. A sacrament of the Christian tradition in which errors or offenses we have committed are acknowledged, with release through the grace of repentance sought. Usually special prayers or acts of goodness are done as penance. Now the "sacrament of reconciliation," though known as "confession" for centuries. A rite of forgiving and invoking healing, as well as new life force to help the initiate proceed on the life journey.

Confirmation. This Christian sacrament is a public rite bearing witness that we are knowledgeable and courageous enough to defend our faith. As a part of the ritual, we are struck (gently) upon the cheek to attest to this inner resolve. Often a spiritual name is chosen, seeking the grace and power the name bestows.

Conflicting thought. A division occurring between heart and mind that creates contradictions between how we think and what we feel.

Confrontation (loving). An imperative of the new era. Part of what we are learning as we reconcile the duality of ourselves and our outer realities. We come to understand the technique called mirroring; by reflecting to one another differing points of understanding, we force integration or separation. Loving confrontation enables us to lift our consciousness to a higher level and bring a new grasp of reality to play in daily life. Loving confrontation can then occur within ourselves as

denial or avoidance is overcome or with others as each grows and provokes the other's growth.

Confucius. b. Lu, Shantung Province, 551 B.C., d. 479. China's most revered moral teacher, philosopher, and statesman. In the careful training of the young men entrusted to his care, he urged them to become models of manhood, possessing *jen*, benevolent love, *shu*, reciprocity, and wisdom. He taught that true manhood means both "to realize the true self and to restore *li*," meaning "rightness, virtue, faith, and proper conduct in all things." *The Analects.*

Consciousness. From two Latin roots, *com* and *scire*, meaning "with knowledge." A state of focused awareness, the level and core of which are directly related to the scope of our attunement to simultaneous processes of life. A registration and response to any impression, through light of the human intellect, operating on the mental plane. Consciousness expands as our intelligence operates on higher levels, with subtler substance and within larger fields. Consciousness is not intellect, rather the result of interaction between intellect and matter–a lighted area in which things are perceived, seen, and sensed; it is created when the intellect of the soul touches matter. While intellect is the positive pole and matter (etheric, physical, astral, and mental) is the negative, consciousness is the lighted area created by their contact. The spark of divinity in the human; the ensouling energy that is the root of all awareness.

Constellation. A group of fixed stars considered to resemble and named after various mythological characters, inanimate objects, and animals. The zodiac consists of twelve constellations contained in the ecliptic–the apparent path of the Sun through the heavens. Due to small periodic motion of the celestial pole of the Earth with respect to the ecliptic pole, the point at which the Sun passes the intersection of the ecliptic and the celestial equator is seen each year in a slightly different position against the stars. Thus the signs, which are measured from the equinox, gradually move away from the constellations whose names they bear and which provide the unmoving sphere against which the vernal point shifts slowly backward. This retrograde movement is called the precession of the equinoxes.

Contemplation. Similar to meditation; the act of holding a thought or object before the mental vision and observing the thought from many perspectives.

Continuity of consciousness. A state of mind or capability linked to the crown CHAKRA for an advanced state when we can slip in and out of the physical body without losing conscious awareness of where we are centered and what we are experiencing, often recognizing two levels of life simultaneously occurring.

Correspondence (Hermetic principle of). One of the HERMETIC PRINCIPLES. "As above, so below" and "Know thyself if you would know another." This law demonstrates the concept of each of us mirroring to one another.

Cosmic consciousness. A profound experience of timelessness that allows us to experience expanded reality; a perspective is experienced from a different point of consciousness than the usual and profoundly changes limited awareness to an expanded outlook.

Cosmic Heart, or Great Heart. An Agni term. The "spiritual heart" of the universe from which pours life-giving emanations of Lots Of

Vital Energy, considered feminine. Mother of the World is but a symbol of this fount of love energy.

Cosmic Magnet. An Agni term. The God consciousness or spiritual high point that remains in place to align all of life in harmony–like Higher Will. When we open to FOHAT, a strong consciousness, a purified heart, and a fiery magnetism develop within us, corresponding in conscious cooperation with the Cosmic Magnet. The teachings tell us this point of consciousness developing within us is the sacred power. Esoteric Christianity would use a term like the Christ-within; in KABALAH the developing inner consciousness would be called DAATH, responding to the Great Magnet of High Consciousness (Cosmic Magnet) that will in time draw all the lower kingdoms into oneness.

Cosmic song. A poetic label given the vibration of the whole cosmos.

Cosmos. The vast space containing all universes, their component solar systems and planets, all material and spiritual existence. While "universe" often refers to the universe of our solar system, cosmos includes all universes.

Coven. A congregation of witches.

Covenant. A promise or commitment; used in spiritual language for its binding power, i.e., the covenant between God and humanity.

Coworkers. Those working in conscious cooperation, vibrating to a harmonious keynote, serving one goal. Spiritually aligned participants in the same vision; a shared state of consciousness in which all workers aligned to the same awareness do their part without hindering the work of the other participants. An alignment of energies toward a higher goal; personalities surrender into the work of the souls as they seek to realize their purpose in the Plan.

Craft, the. A commonly used synonym for Wicca, or witchcraft.

Creative workers. A category of world servers who work through integrated head, heart, sacral, and root chakras to step down the higher Plan for humanity.

Crosses. *See pages 43-44.*

Crown. To esoteric traditions this symbolizes the highest CHAKRA, correlating to the Egyptian headwear, the Native American headdress of feathers, the antler horns on Viking and Mongolian helmets, the elaborate

Crosses of the World

Ankh. This cross of ancient Egypt symbolizes the energy pattern of the human body and means "life."

Cross, Botonnee. With arms ending in a graceful trefoil design that suggests the Holy Trinity, the popular Botonnee cross has been widely used on royal and aristocratic coats-of-arms as a reminder of service to humanity and to God. To kabalists the top TREFOIL represents the highest three SEPHIROTH and the long, vertical bar, the descent to Malkuth, the kingdom of matter, signifying that our work is to bring the kingdom of God to Earth.

Cross, Celtic. The original Celtic crosses were found in Great Britain and Ireland where they were erected as wayside and cemetery crosses. The circle is an emblem of life everlasting, no beginning and no end. The Celtic cross is also known as the Cross of Iona because it is thought to have been taken by Celtic Christians from Ireland to the Island of Iona in the 6th century, before the Roman arm of Christianity arrived.

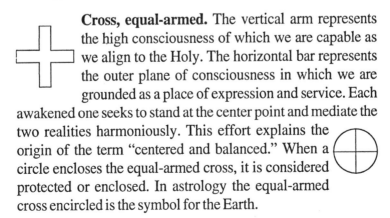

Cross, equal-armed. The vertical arm represents the high consciousness of which we are capable as we align to the Holy. The horizontal bar represents the outer plane of consciousness in which we are grounded as a place of expression and service. Each awakened one seeks to stand at the center point and mediate the two realities harmoniously. This effort explains the origin of the term "centered and balanced." When a circle encloses the equal-armed cross, it is considered protected or enclosed. In astrology the equal-armed cross encircled is the symbol for the Earth.

Cross, Jerusalem. A specialized form of the Cross Cantonnee, which consists of a central cross surrounded by four smaller crosses of the same design. The five crosses symbolize the five steps of initiation in the Christian path. Like the five-pointed star, we are reminded of dedicating the physical, emotional, mental,  spiritual, and social aspects of our lives to the Christ when masterhood of personality is complete and spiritualized consciousness is realized.

Cross, rose. A single rose marks the cross arms designating the heart center on this simple cross. Rosicrucians use this single rose on a cross as their symbol.

Cross with seven roses. This Western symbol of seven roses entwining the vertical bar of the cross represents the seven chakras on the human body opening and releasing their spiritual powers in the same way the depiction of the lotus on the human body serves the East.

feather dressings for the Maya. This head ornamentation is a sign of high consciousness, awakened leadership, one with God–victory, majesty, sovereignty, and dominion. A symbol of Christ the King to Christians.

Crystallization. Definite or permanent in form. Stabilization or fixation of thoughts, ideas, or physical realities into dense form or at a lower rate of vibration. Ac-cording to the law of fixation that governs the mental plane, the result of crystallization is an inevitable shattering so that the indwelling life can be freed for further progress.

Crystals. Various qualities are attributed to gemstones. Their powers and healing properties are being studied and used by many for their transformational effects.

Cult. A body of believers gathered around a charismatic leader, attracted by a personality to which obsessive devotion is projected. A standard cult characteristic is "sameness"–lack of individuality. Members must adhere to a strong belief system, behavior is dictated and must conform, expectations of routine are defined, and allegiance is expected or commanded. A cult is empowered primarily by the strong allegiance that binds the organization or group. The cult concept is anathema to free thinkers or occultists.

Cusp. The transitional first or last part of an astrological house or sign. The period when two signs overlap–creating an intensified period of energy. In an ASTROLOGY chart, the sign found on each house demarcation which, with its ruling planet, affects or modifies the activities of the house. Events that occur or planets that reside within the last or first degrees of a sign are affected by the energies of both the sign of actual placement and the proximate sign. Astrologers find there are significant challenges for those born near a change of signs or within the cusp period. Each sign contains 30 degrees: 0 degrees of any sign will express that sign most radically; 29 degrees of any sign

intensifies the need to display the qualities or influences of that given sign. Each person is evolving into his or her native Sun sign and so must attempt consciously to build the faculties of that sign.

Cyberspace. The destruction or breakdown of fixed time and space identities. As people from one part of the world relate to others, the question of time and distance begin to dissolve. All of us have thoughtforms built of separate realities; cyberspace demands we merge and acknowledge that we know of tomorrow's events today if we are talking to someone on the other side of the dateline.

Cycle. Astrologically, the orbit of a celestial body; a time interval in which it completes a revolution around another body on a regular basis. Each planet adheres to its particular cycle, dependent upon the speed of the planet and the distance it travels to complete an orbit, e.g., the Moon takes approximately 28 days to complete one cycle, the Earth takes about 365 days to orbit the Sun, and the Sun approximately 365 days to complete one cycle of the zodiac (28-30 days each to pass through the twelve zodiacal signs). Also, all life is cyclic, in accord to the principle, "as above, so below." Just as planetary cycles exist, so do the rhythms and cycles of human life, seasons of the years–"what goes around, comes around." With wisdom applied, gentle shifts can be achieved.

D

 Daath. Kabalistic term for the consciousness of the individual soul's evolutionary pattern, portrayed on the kabalistic Tree of Life as a dotted circle for those who have incarnated but have not as yet achieved completion. Gnosis and Sophia have the same meaning: wisdom evolving.

Daily review. *See* Nightly review.

Dalai Lama. The title means "Exalted Ocean." The current spiritual leader of Tibetan Buddhism, b. Takster, 1935, is now in exile in India. He was designated 14th Dalai Lama in 1937 by the Gelugpa order of monks of Lhasa, who were convinced he was the reincarnation of the Compassionate Buddha. Forced into exile after China's savage suppression of the Tibetan National Uprising of 1959, he remains the spiritual and temporal head of Tibet–an eloquent and unique spokesman for Buddhism around the world.

Dark night of the soul. A painful period of testing when the soul must stand alone and test its own strength or light.

Death. The most commonly used term for shedding the physical form. The great misunderstanding of life stems from ignorance, for death is confused with the "end." Indeed, birth is death (entering limitation), and death is birth (a return to our spirit nature).

Déjà vu. A conscious experience of "knowing" that something is familiar and has been experienced before; recalled from another point of time and space. It is a phenomenon similar to lucid dreaming but occurs in an awakened state.

Delusion. Distortion in the astral nature that blinds human beings to their real nature. The "unreal" through which we must pierce to perceive the greater values life offers.

Demiurge. The leader of the archons, a second-rate deity who falsely imagines himself to be the true God and claims creation of the world of appearances.

Demon. An evil entity that has never had a human form but establishes contact with a human being. The term denotes a negative influence on human beings so affected.

Dense body. The physical body.

Dense world. The lowest subplane of the physical world; commonly, physical reality which consists of matter visible to the human eye. To many, the "real world."

Descent into matter. The soul enveloped into denser and denser realities culminating in a physical or materialized result.

Desirelessness. A term used in Eastern thought to encourage nonattachment to material reality so that spiritual reality may emerge more clearly.

Devachan. A Sanskrit term. The heavenly world where weary souls rest, refresh the spirit, and experience no pain in a spirit reality.

Devas. Also called "angels," these comprise a parallel evolution to humanity and often interact. Devic forces, often called the "builders of form," command many forces of nature. They work with the lesser kingdoms evolving on Earth and cowork effectively with humans of stable temperament and advanced in understanding spiritual law. Devas usually guide the work of elementals, serving humanity and more advanced angels on a line of hierarchical advancement. Much work has been undertaken to counterbalance man's 5000 years of unconsciousness. Now this force must be invoked consciously by human beings advanced enough to summon, wisely and respectfully, the forces of these creative fires.

Dharma. The way of high character, duty, or purpose; our mission in life; a reason for being; service to the Plan, to God, to Planetary Logos. Used to denote the positive forces we have earned to help us meet well the experience of life; sometimes called "good karma."

Dharma Light. An Eastern term for the outpouring of the mind, love, and will of God; the grace of God's Light poured forth upon the

Earth–"divine Light." A guiding principle: the law, love, and wisdom that hold all things together and are essential to both happiness and progress along the spiritual path. The inner mystical light experienced by the soul on its journey through the higher realms. Dharma implies law and is derived from the root *dhri:* to hold, to support, to sustain, or to bear. Universal ethical conduct or the true, correct, and wisely chosen fulfillment of obligations sometimes considered the duty–religious or moral–of humanity. *See* the Cloud of Knowable Things.

Dhyani-Chohans. A Sanskrit Tibetan compound term meaning "Lords of Meditation." Great beings devoted to contemplating, unfolding, and fulfilling the divine Plan. Conscious, intelligent powers in nature divinely charged with the supervision of the cosmos. Generally speaking, any celestial being who has advanced to a stage superior to the human kingdom. Frequently a specific planetary spirit acting as regent of a planet or planetary chain. Traditionally, Dhyani-Chohans are divided into three major classes or kingdoms–each of which is subdivided into seven sub-classes. They comprise the collective hosts of spiritual beings–the angels of Christianity, the ELOHIM and "messengers" of Judaism–the means for the manifestation of the divine or universal mind and creative will. This wondrous group of beings has evolved through the Earth life chain in former world periods and now acts as guides, lords, leaders, and saviors of evolving human and planetary life.

Discarnates. That part of the human kingdom not presently embodied in physical form but existing in nonphysical dimensions. Human beings who have made their transition from Earth-plane life to dwell for a time in the nonphysical realms.

Discernment. A GIFT OF THE SPIRIT, achieved after much interaction between conscious mind and higher consciousness. This goal of the disciple is realized as the energy of the soul from its level and the higher mind blend in new awareness.

Disciple. In esoteric tradition, specifically a first- or second-degree initiate. In common usage, a pupil or follower who helps spread a Master's teachings. Those who follow a particular discipline according to a prescribed pattern but also recog-

nize much free will and understanding. Those subscribing to a constant habit of spiritual living whose knowledge, capacities, and spiritual abilities are demonstrated in daily life.

Disease (or dis-ease). Disharmony between levels of self which results in a breakdown of health in any of the personality sheaths.

Distance healing. Techniques to bring about healing that may be used without the patient being physically present.

Divination. The use of nonphysical senses or intuition to know that which is not apparent to the five senses. The art of foretelling future events or revealing hidden knowledge by means of psychic or physical tools.

Divine discontent. That impulse within us which awakens as consciousness begins to sense that "there is more to life than meets the eye." A restlessness of spirit that irritates personality to keep it searching for deeper understanding.

Divine feminine. The feminine aspect of God, often called the "Mother," especially aspects of love, sensitivity, and nurturing, concerned with protection and the perfection of intuition.

Divine Principle. An Agni term meaning God or the Creator. A substitute term rising out of the suppression of religion under communism. The word "God," offensive to the new Soviet regime, was disallowed. New terms served to some degree, but the teachings of Agni Yoga were nonetheless kept hidden, veiled in the love of culture and art, spoken of only in terms of culture.

Divine realization. Moments of revelation merging into synthesis or comprehension.

Dogma. Specific tenets of a religious sect. Adherents are obligated to accept these as creed to receive grace.

Dogwood. The flower that blooms at the Easter season resembling a cross. Each petal bears a mark very like a blood-stained nailprint. Its center suggests the crown of thorns. Legend has it that the crucifix was hewn of dogwood. Now the tree grows slight of trunk, not thick enough to support a body.

Dominions. Angels of an advanced order who will the PLAN of God and obey the THRONES. They are responsible for the economy of nature and work as agents of supply and demand. They regulate activities and duties of the angels.

Dove. The descending dove is the most widely used symbol of the Holy Spirit. At Jesus' baptism "the Holy Spirit descended on him, like a dove, and a voice from  heaven, saying, "You are my beloved Son; with you I am pleased." (Luke 3.22) The dove is also the symbol for Sophia.

Dowsing. "Water witching." A nonscientific method of receiving information from spiritual sources through techniques understood by the operator as attunement. Used for locating Earth energy leys, underground water, lost articles, and specific answers. The American Dowsers Society, Danville, Vermont 05828, is a recognized authority on this phenomenon.

Dream. A drama presented by an altered state of consciousness to convey meaning to the rational mind of the dreamer. Esotericists consider dreams to be highly significant and worthy of study to uncover disguised meaning. *See* Freud, Sigmund; Jung, Carl.

Dreaming, lucid. An explicit awareness while in the dream state that we are dreaming. We are not awake, yet often we discover we are able to control the dream, its nature, or its outcome as we desire. This deliberate act of taking control demonstrates the empowerment of the dreamer. Tibetan Masters call it "dreaming true," a level of high spiritual consciousness where wisdom and knowledge are accessible.

Druid. The intelligentsia of the Celtic tradition. From this group of scholars came the chiefs, judges, and magicians (shamans) to teach the immortality of the soul and reincarnation. In Glastonbury, England, they

Mistletoe, sacred plant of Druids

still believe Jesus studied with the Druids before returning to be baptized (by John) and to begin his ministry.

Dugpas. Testing agents residing within the ego that resist light and seek to slow those on the path. The symbology of good and bad angels represents challenges presented by devas of light and dugpas–dark elementals of self-service that must be aligned to the soul purpose before advancement on the initiatory path can occur. Dugpas are often called "evil" because they work on the path of involution, rather than evolution.

Dweller on the Threshold. The individual, as well as collective, unfinished business that impedes our human spiritual advancement. This negative configuration has been labeled "the devil"–as in "the devil made me do it." A symbolic name for the collection of unique imperfections (old selves) with which each of us struggles. The sum-total of all that personality holds and its defects–the potencies (physical, emotional, and mental) which limit the expression of the soul. The works of CARL JUNG and ROBERTO ASSAGIOLI help us become conscious of the SHADOW or unknown parts of ourselves. Both Jungian psychology and Assagioli's PSYCHOSYNTHESIS acknowledge the personality and the spiritual nature of each person and the need for the various parts of the self to function as a harmonious whole.

E

Earth religion. Any religion which has as its basic tenet that all life is sacred and connected, honoring nature as the embodiment of divinity. Its practices seek to bring the individual into harmony with the Earth, its natural cycles, and the rhythms of the universe as sources of spiritual wisdom and experiences of union with the divine. Such religions oppose the idea that the world is to be subdued and its resources exploited.

Earthborn paradises. Places prepared in the astral dimension for those not yet mature enough to enjoy the heavens of the inner world, i.e., playgrounds for young or immature souls unprepared for spiritual training. They will abide there until they evolve into states of inner life that will have meaning.

Earth energies. Leys, or currents, in the Earth that flow in recognizable patterns to vitalize sites for spiritual purposes. These are detectable by dowsers or sensitives.

Easter. The celebration of the resurrection of Jesus, the historical Christ. It is a time full of joy and profound meaning for all Christians. When Jesus reappeared after the entombment, his friends knew his death was not final. A movable Christian celebration set by a religious formula: In the Roman Catholic Church, Easter is the first Sunday after the full moon following spring equinox. In the Byzantine tradition, Easter is calculated differently and often follows the Easter Sunday of the Western tradi-

tion. One of three major spiritual festivals of the year, the Aries full moon is a time of welcoming the new annual cycle–a festival of renewal, resurrection, and reconstruction. The cross of the Risen Christ will be the symbol of the forthcoming era. Each springtime, nature demonstrates how beautiful new life can spring from something that seems to have died.

Eastern Orthodoxy. The Eastern division of the early church when it divided into two factions in A.D. 1054, becoming the Roman Catholic and the Eastern Orthodox Church.

Ecclesiast. Literally, "a person who is a member of an assembly *(ecclesia)*" or who takes part in the discussions of a learned group.

Ectoplasm. The ethers, or energy, of the etheric body of a medium used in the manifestation of an apparition, especially as used in seances.

Educare. Latin root word from which *education* derives. Literal meaning, "to lead out," as from ignorance or darkness.

Educators of the new age. A category of world servers who work through integrated head, ajna, and throat chakras to step down the higher Plan for humanity.

ego (with lower-case e). The personality yet to be prepared or sufficiently trained for spirituality; the self-centered, self-satisfied point of consciousness not yet able to release its fascination with the false identity.

Ego (with a capital E). Latin for "I" meaning individualized self-consciousness; the perfect self that experiences in form and animates the will of human life; the developing, unfolding human soul. This reincarnating self is the lower representative of the monadic vehicle and exists on the plane of abstract intellect, storing the knowledge and experiences of all incarnations. Ego is the divine Self that gathers sheaths about itself as it descends into the world of lower vibration.

Egotism. A psychological term for excessive self-involvement; a barrier to spiritual growth because the nonself claims the power of identity and denies the true self participation in life experiences; thus, the self is blocked and cannot contribute to self-evolution.

Eight-fold Path. BUDDHA'S teaching of the way of the Middle Path. These are disciplines to be exercised in specific areas of life to attain release from the wheel of rebirth. He summarized the conditions of life in his FOUR NOBLE TRUTHS. He taught that the way to escape sorrow is by obedience to the Eight-fold Path: right-belief, right-thought, right-speech, right-action, right-livelihood, right-endeavor, right-remembrance, right-medita-tion/concentration.

Elder Brothers (before the Throne). A biblical reference to those who have evolved through the human experience and now serve as guides to human-ity–saints, sages, and holy ones who guide and guard those evolving by the same route, assisting them to become wise and preparing them for tests ahead. We might call their service "divine parenting." These guardians of humanity have inspired the wisdom teachings and designed ancient and modern ceremonials to assist all on the spiritual path. Sincere aspirants are watched over and may receive aid from humanity's elder brethren, members of the Brotherhood of the Adepts. Serving humanity in many ways, they assure compassion and effective care, especially through periods of darkness in human history. *See* Brotherhood.

Elemental forces. Basic building blocks of earth, air, water, and fire used in the creation and maintenance of the physical world. These forces have specific roles. They are the forces behind the outer forms guiding evolution through interplay. Wise Ones work through a hierarchy of responsibility constructed to allow growth at every level.

Elemental world. Patterns of lower evolution are everywhere about and within the personality waiting to be confronted by the purification process. These energies of body, emotion, and mind are maintained by the combined work of elementals who will be acted upon by the evolving consciousness.

Elementals. Also known as Spirits of the Elements, Nature Spirits, Terrestrial Spirits, or Elemental Principles. The guiding awareness of each group-mind forming the natural (or nature) forces of earth (gnomes), air (sylphs), water (undines), and fire (salamanders). These entities pursue their evolutionary experience prior to assuming a physical or material form. Three elemental kingdoms must be passed through before entering into the more advanced group of the mineral kingdom. These forces are subhuman and are on the path of involution, or the downward arc. Although they can be contacted on the emotional (astral) plane, controlled and harnessed through the use of various rites and ceremonies, it is advised they be handled with great care. These intelligences form the link between the parts and the consciousness of the unit, energy field, or standing wave patterns. They can be acknowledged and come to coworking relationship in *magick* and shamanism.

Elohim. The Old Testament Hebrew term for the gods (plural) of creation, who proclaimed, "Let us make man in our image, after our likeness." (Genesis 1.26)

Emotional body. The vehicle, or reflective nature, occultly called "astral" (meaning "starry") wherein reside unresolved emotions and currents of force awaiting expression.

Energy. An oft-used, modern term for the forces of life at work throughout creation. As humanity becomes increasingly sensitive to unseen forces and the vibration of the environment, these undifferentiated currents are being collectively labeled "energy."

Energy biocircuit. The interplay of forces and energies circulating through the meridians, chakras, and nadis of the etheric body. Not easy to measure by physical means, but recognized for centuries in natural healing, acupuncture, and acupressure therapies.

Enlightenment. Supreme discrimination; a state of mind filled with spiritual wisdom. Salvation.

Enneagram. This ancient metaphysical system popularized by G. Gurdjieff and adopted for modern application defines personality types based on the number 9, the forgotten 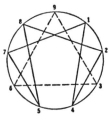 basis for most systems of numerology. More recently, it has been elaborated upon by Jungian psychologists.

Enthusiasm. The Agni virtue for Aries. "The fire of Theos" that ignites within us and animates our being with higher waves of consciousness. Contagious enthusiasm ignites the spirit of another when it flares and expresses. Those filled with enthusiasm transmit enthusiasm.

Entities. Discarnates, or spirit beings, without physical bodies that can be seen or recognized by some but are undetectable by others. They continue to live in an appropriate dimension between physical incarnations. Some visitation and contact between planes is noted; their presence may be positive or negative.

Entities, attached. Spirits (discarnates) that attach to the aura, sphere, or body from past lives or this life and need to be released. They are seeking sensations and feelings that cannot be found in the higher planes. They may not know anything about traveling to another dimension or even that they are dead; they are responding to cravings or instincts of an addictive nature. PSYCHOGRAPHY or other EXORCISM rites are used to facilitate spirit releasement.

Ephemeris. A scientific table of coordinates used to indicate the daily positions of the planets, stars, and celestial bodies as they traverse the heavens.

Epiphany. This season starts with Epiphany Day, January 6, and continues until Lent. We remember that the Magi, the three wisemen, saw a great star and, after traveling in its direction, found the baby Jesus. Even though Jesus was a Jewish baby, his smile and his love were for them also. The Magi were Gentiles. So we may believe God loves ALL people. Epiphany Day is white, but the rest of the season is green, symbolizing the growth of love among all God's people.

Equinox. Either of two points on the celestial sphere where the ecliptic intersects with the celestial equator. The two times during each year when the Sun crosses the celestial equator and the lengths of day and night are approximately equal. The vernal equinox and the autumnal equinox denote the changing of the seasons to spring and fall, respectively. At the time of the spring equinox the Sun enters Aries (the first sign of the zodiac), and at the time of the fall equinox the Sun enters Libra.

Era of Woman. Esoteric teachings refer to the Aquarian Age as a time to balance the nature (masculine-feminine) of humanity through awakening to the values of the feminine influence. *See* Roerich, Helena.

Eros. In Greek mythology, the God of Love, the son of Aphrodite. The sum total of the human instincts of self-preservation–more specifically, love of a sexual or instinctual nature. The aggregate of pleasure-directed life instincts whose energy is derived from the libido. Self-fulfilling love.

Esbat. Monthly meeting of a coven most often held at full Moon (of which there are usually thirteen each year). Some groups also meet at the dark of the Moon.

Esoteric. The Greek root *eso* means "within." That which is hidden, unseen, or secret. An inner, or out-of-sight, process. Obscure teachings meaningful to those spiritually prepared to receive them. In the New Testament, Jesus spoke of teachings reserved only for disciples which he did not offer the public. His exoteric, or public, teachings were parables which, though commonly understood, also contained other and deeper meanings.

Esoteric anatomy. A study of the body beyond its concrete form, especially the "organs" of the nonphysical body–chakras, etc.–as well as the body in other realms of being, such as astral, etheric, mental, etc.

Esoteric astrology. The study of astrology that recognizes the soul and its work behind the scene of personality and the hidden or inner reasons for life.

Esoteric Christianity. The Christian tradition contains both esoteric and exoteric levels of understanding. The esoteric focuses upon developing the Christ-within and the gifts of the spirit, as referred to in the New Testament; esoteric Christianity, equivalent to mystical Christianity, emphasizes keys to the inner nature or soul development. Exoteric Christianity focuses upon dogma and rites, the better understood practices of the church tradition.

Esoteric doctrine. An inner interpretation of perspectives on life.

Esoteric philosophy. A perspective emphasizing inner life and practices to enhance understanding of the soul's purpose.

Esoteric psychology. These teachings emphasize the inner knowledge, disciplines, and practices concerning the science of the soul. The Rays are considered significant factors of esoteric psychology.

Essenes. One of several sects of Jews living near Jerusalem at the time of Jesus. Popular opinion in metaphysical thought is that Jesus was a practicing Essene.

Etheric body. The form of ethers that interfaces the physical and nonphysical realities. The four ethers are known as (from lower to higher) chemical, life, light, reflecting.

Etheric plane. The region of the physical world consisting of four ethers of subtle matter less dense than the three lower levels of the physical world. The physical world is divided into seven sub-planes, and the four highest sub-planes together are called the etheric plane, or SUBTLE BODY. Physical form is modeled or patterned after the densified spirit of the etheric plane. Also, having to do with the frequencies penetrating into and beyond Earth's physical atmosphere and interfacing Earth with the astral world.

Ethers. A substance with frequencies that interpenetrate and move more rapidly in vibration than matter. A more subtle, reflective material of our atmosphere less dense than physical matter and through which the spiritual model of life-forms communicates to the physical form.

 Ethical living. *See* Yoga, Agni.

Ethics. The code or philosophy we develop and adopt that protects personal integrity, that path of rightness for peace of mind and established harmony between inner and outer.

Eucharist. *See* Communion, Holy.

Eurythmy. A specific system of physical movements–not unlike TAI CHI–taught by RUDOLF STEINER as health-building and healing.

Evil. The current or action of life that moves us away from the soul's purpose and direction, against the natural current toward evolution and soul-fulfillment. The power of that which is from the past and, though obsolete, still persists, seeking to prevent progress. Opposite pole of evolution; that which hinders soul purpose when on the evolutionary arc.

As an Agni term: That which is resistant to evolutionary forces. The resistant ego that refuses to accept the light of high consciousness, choosing instead to embrace the forces of darkness.

Evocation. The coming forth of energy or spirit in response to an invocation. God may evoke us; we may evoke lower spirits or elementals.

Evolution. The progressive march toward a higher life. The natural, unfolding development of latent potential within all life, guided by an inherent design. The process of liberation of spirit from the restriction of form. For humanity, the process of awakening to the plan and purpose of God, expanding in consciousness, and attaining, stage by stage, an ever more inclusive awareness. (Evolution of the planet is linked uniquely to human evolution as humanity is the *manas,* or mind, for planetary life. Planet Earth evolves as value systems of planet life sensitize to purposes of the Logos.)

Evolutions, other. Three parallel evolutions are developing through the life of our planet: human, spacial, angelic. Each is centered on a specific plane of existence and evolves into others. For example, humans are centered on the physical and evolve into emotional, mental, and higher dimensions. *See individual entries.*

Existentialism. An attitude or philosophy concerning the fate of humanity and the individual which emphasizes free will and taking responsibility for the consequences of our acts.

Exorcism. A technique to release a possessing spirit from a human being and advance the possessing entity into the light. *See* Spirit releasement therapy.

Exoteric. From the Greek root *exo,* meaning "outside." The opposite of esoteric, or hidden. Popular religious teachings given openly and publicly. The Christian church has traditionally emphasized the exoteric message of its faith, dogma, while neglecting the mystery side of the Christian teachings. *See* Esoteric Christianity.

Expanded awareness. A state of consciousness in which we sense more than what is readily recognizable through the physical senses or is grasped by the rational mind. The heightened ability to directly perceive and experience subtle truths and realities as they exist in both the subjective and objective worlds. The ability to perceive from the world of causes in which we increasingly identify with divine will.

Expanded Sense Perception (also known as ESP, or Extrasensory Perception). The utilization of the astral senses in gathering impressions or information, i.e., clairsentience, clairaudience, and clairvoyance.

Expanding vehicles. Vehicles of consciousness–means of knowing–hold a line of tension between two poles (spirit and matter). As we gain more mastery of the abilities of each body, each is brought under control, tested, and found valuable to this evolving soul. The existing ability extends to broader expression.

Expansion of consciousness. Progression of consciousness from one level to another as our awareness of personal and planetary purpose increases. Ability to function effectively on more advanced planes of being or from higher states of consciousness. The registration and assimilation of energies that allow us to build new relationships and to extend our fields of perception and activity.

As an Agni term: the ability to perceive from a higher and broader perspective, realizing the ability to free ourselves from a limited point of identity by moving to a wider window of perspective. The ability to perceive from a number of perspectives instead of being locked into one identity, i.e., the ego, or nonself.

Externalization of the Hierarchy. Name given by MASTER DJWHAL KHUL through Alice A. BAILEY for the return of the disciples and Masters, as well as the Christ, to the world of denser vibration and a new round of incarnations by teachers and saints, whereby they will work closely with humanity to prepare for collective initiations and the planetary initiation. This return is imminent.

Extrasensory perception (ESP). The nonphysical senses that may be developed and used to gather information in nontraditional ways. Also called "extended sense awareness."

Eye of Horus. An Egyptian symbol representing the spiritual eye of the illumined. In the Egyptian mystery tradition the Utchat, the "all-seeing" eye, refers to the Pole Star and to illumination; the eye of the mind. The eye of Horus may be associated with the Moon and its phases. An image of the eye of God was buried with the dead to symbolize God accompanying the deceased's spirit on the dark journey through the underworld.

Eye of Taurus. A symbol representing the spiritual eye of the illumined, of pre-Egyptian origin, and associated with the Age of Taurus. Literally, the great star Aldebran which shines forth as the eye of the Bull; the great Light considered to be the source of the intuitional or buddhic plane within the constellation of Taurus, the Bull. Also symbolic of the energy of the enlightened one, the great Lord Buddha, rushing into manifestation with great light and power. This energy radiates for a moment from the soul of the disciple who enters into the awareness of the intuitional or buddhic plane characterized by pure reason, understanding, and enlightenment.

F

Familial love. From the Greek *philia*. Family or brotherly love. The bonds of emotion that link two or more people through blood ties, tribal bonds, or nationalism.

Fear. A most serious obstacle to spiritual growth. Fear indicates lack of trust and a lack of belief in the goodness of the higher Plan. Fear is a major destructive component of the DWELLER ON THE THRESHOLD.

☿ **Fearlessness.** Agni virtue for Capricorn. Since fear blocks, this virtue is designed to support the energy of life as it moves through creation. Courage is essential for the spiritual aspirant who dares to interact with unknown forces. Fearlessness results as we identify with the highest and release our identity with the false.

Feathered Serpent. An archetype of Mesoamerican traditions, recognizing that spirit which is held imprisoned in matter and crawls upon the Earth may be uplifted to higher consciousness and ascend with spirit. The snake itself symbolizes timeless time, or life inching forward eternally, containing wisdom, consciously or unconsciously. *See* Ourobourus; Quetzalcoatl.

Feminine principle. The feminine aspect of God called SHAKTI, in human form, but hidden within all matter and gradually evolving planetary life. Having been dormant in the recent period, the feminine principle is awakening to bring her realizations and increased intuition to humanity.

Feng Shui. Known as the "art of placement," this classic Chinese form of GEOMANCY demonstrates overt and obscure ways the physical ambience–home and workplace, environment and landscape–can spark and nurture the natural potential to be more alive, receptive, and focused. This technique concerns itself with the moving energy called *chi,* directing it to affect the environment by balancing YIN/YANG into a harmonious flow according to the purpose to which a space is dedicated.

Festival of the Christ. One of three major spiritual festivals of the year. A celebration at Gemini full moon recognizing the Christ within humankind. This festival celebrates the spirit of humanity aspiring toward God, seeking alignment with divine will according to the Christ pattern, and dedicated to right human relations. Also known as the Festival of Humanity, the Festival of Goodwill, World Invocation Day, and the Christ's Festival.

 Fiery impulse. An Agni term. The impelling force within that impels us to strive for oneness toward the primary Source. These forces, natural to the ascent of consciousness, are to be guarded and valued. Without honoring these saturations, we lose our vitality. Each fiery impulse is respected and appreciated because it empowers the spirit in its quest.

Fiery world. An Agni Yoga term for the world of FOHAT, higher vibration where the "fire" of God is more pronounced, more intense.

Fifth kingdom (of Souls). A new state of collective consciousness not yet manifested, although the model has been created as a divine potential by Master Jesus and other MASTERS. When enough humans can sustain the collective energy, the initiation will be granted and a leap forward in consciousness will be gained by many now in preparation. (The other four kingdoms are the mineral, the plant, the animal, the human.) Corresponds to the "Kingdom of God" in the New Testament.

Financiers and economists. A category of world servers who work through integrated head, heart, throat, and sacral chakras to step down the higher plan for humanity.

Fire; Flames. In symbology, representative of the HOLY SPIRIT, martyrdom, and religious fervor. Also, a symbol of Agni, "fire of purification."

Fire mysteries. A Christian term for Easter mysteries. The intensity builds as we are subjected to the fire of purification, being tempered and tried so that all that is not of the higher is burned away.

Fires of Space. An Agni term. The cosmic blending of the fusion of sparks precipitated by the Cosmic Magnet. Fiery seeds live in each atom, and the power of cohesion rests in these fiery seeds. When the intensified force of the creative magnet is acting, the fire of the seed fuses with the impulsion of the COSMIC MAGNET. The manifested fire breathes into the impulse of fire in each atom; thus the spirit of creativity is enlivened.

Firewalk. A phenomenon wherein a person, in an altered state of consciousness, actually and physically walks barefooted, without harm, on a bed of coals. This practice is found throughout the world in a variety of cultures, but within the last twenty years has been introduced to middle-class America as proof of and exposure to the power of altered states of mind.

Fixed design. These words from the "I Am the Soul" mantra refer to the parts of us which are "fixed" on the time/space level, e.g., our parentage, race, birth date and place, sex, culture–as compared to those evolutionary potentials of personality, heart, and mind. When we voice, "I am fixed design," we are affirming, "I am stationed at a particular point and I accept that–I can do it!"

Fohat. An Agni term. A Sanskrit word for the subtlest fiery energy of creation, also called atomic energy, a reference to the atmic plane. In some writings it is referred to as "actually omnipresent fire"; Helena uses the term as "psychic energy" in *Letters of Helena Roerich.* Fire and energy often are equated in these writings, somewhat as in Kabalah. Fohat is referred to as "primary energy" and "cosmic electricity" as well–always respectfully addressed as the beginning of attraction and the electric power of affinity and sympathy, as manifested in the pure spirit. Fohat then is the *prima materia* –cosmic substance–out of which all is initiated into manifestation. Striving prepares us for contact with fohat. The fiery spirit called "Father" would be fohat, which corresponds to Chokmah on the kabalistic TREE OF LIFE. Said H.P. BLAVATSKY, "Fohat is the steed, and thought is the rider."

Fohat/Materia Lucida. A combined Agni term. Fohat as the energy aspect of primal energy-matter and MATERIA LUCIDA as luminous matter are contrasted beautifully in the following quote from *Agni Yoga* (144). "Nurturing the psychic energy, Fohat paves the way to the far-off worlds. Whereas, Materia Lucida weaves the strengthening of the consciousness. One strengthens, the other forces one into the depthless pit of perfectionment."

Fornication. A word used in the Bible referring to the misapplication of spiritual power or violation of right action.

Fortune, Dion. b. Wales, 1890, d. 1946. Author, teacher, and founder of the Society of the Inner Light dedicated to the study of the Western esoteric traditions, particularly meditation and personal regeneration. *The Training and Work of an Initiate*, 1930; *Esoteric Philosophy of Love and Marriage*, 4th edition, 1967; *The Cosmic Doctrine*, 1966; biography by Janine Chapman: *Quest for Dion Fortune,* 1993.

Four Noble Truths. Part of the principal teachings of Lord Guatama, the BUDDHA, who lived about 500 years before Jesus, the Christ. The Four Noble Truths are: all life is suffering; the cause of sorrow is desire (addictions); escape from sorrow comes when all selfish thought ceases; and the way to escape sorrow is obedience to the EIGHT-FOLD PATH.

Freedom. An Agni theme. A discipline which is realized when our consciousness guides, leads, and directs the life, rather than instinct, urges, glamour, or illusion. Freedom to be the true self–clear and clean–is the goal; change and constant adjustment become the way. Advancement and self-discipline clear the way so we may be all that we can be. Correlates to the energy and influence of the number 5. As an Agni term: A state of being in which we are constantly moving toward a greater and greater overcoming of the RINGS-PASS-NOT of consciousness, overcoming all sense of limitation, that oneness with COSMIC CONSCIOUSNESS may be realized.

Freemasonry. An international secret fraternity, Free and Accepted Masons, originating in medieval England. Its ritualistic elements, such as initiations, derived from the mystery religions.

Freud, Sigmund. b. Moravia, 1856, d. 1939. Austrian physician and neurologist whose analytic work with Joseph Breuer led him to the belief that symptoms with no physiological basis could be alleviated by hypnosis and thus had a psychogenic basis. His *Studies in Hysteria* marked the beginning of the psychoanalysis movement. He conceived the tripartite division of the unconscious mind as id, ego, superego and postulated that dreams, like neuroses, are disguised manifestations of repressed desires and the "royal road to the unconscious." In later life, recognizing the limitations of traditional psychotherapies, he expressed interest in Transcendental Meditation as a technique for relieving psychic suffering. *The Interpretation of Dreams,* 1900; *The Ego and the Id*, 1923; *The Future of an Illusion*, 1927.

Full Moon. The phase of the Moon when fully illuminated, reflecting most powerfully the light of the Sun.

Full Moon meditation. A ritual, meditation, or celebration wherein participants choose to receive the blessings of the spiritual hierarchy associated with a given Sun sign period. Those gathered respond consciously to the unique opportunity for expansion in awareness provided by the hierarchical influ-

ence of the ruling constellation during the Full Moon period as the time of peak exposure to the Sun's light. Some are also beginning to call these Full Moon meditations Sun Sign festivals.

Fundamentalism. A term used to describe the philosophy of those who affirm the fundamental truths of a religious approach. However, the term has come to denote a literal translation, not the true meaning.

Future. An Agni theme. To direct the consciousness into the future is the aim of a true school. When we think of ourselves as "on the cutting edge," we are in the formation of the guiding influence. We must recognize that today is the foundation for tomorrow. Correlates to the energy and influence of the number 4.

G

Gaia. The Greek name for the goddess Terra, the uninitiated Earth.

Gaia hypothesis. A modern grasp of planetary life as one entity wherein all species are coordinated and interacting for the well being of the whole, the planet. This effective system is becoming clearer with more modern scientific tracking now possible to see how systemic are the functions of the planet–water, winds, pollution, all kingdoms.

Gandhi, Mohandas, Mahatma. Great Soul. b. Porbandar, India, 1869, d. 1948. Great moral teacher and reformer–not only of his homeland but of the world. The embodiment of the principle of *ahimsa,* harmlessness, he became "the almost mystical incarnation of nationhood...and exemplar of soul-force to achieve righteous ends by non-violent civil disobedience." He said that underlying all that is ever-changing, ever-dying is "a Living Power that is changeless, that holds all together, that creates, dissolves, and recreates. That informing Power or Spirit is God." Gandhi believed that only in times of true silence was one capable of experiencing God's mercy.

Gender (Hermetic principle of). "All things have gender": masculine and feminine at work to balance, rejuvenate, or be made whole. Respect for gender is necessary for generation; lack of respect causes degeneration.

Gene pool. A collection of genetic possibilities that can exist individually for one person or collectively for humanity, as well as other species.

General Good. An Agni term for Higher Plan.

Geomancy. An ancient study of right relationship between sacred structures, the sites upon which they are located, lines of magnetism, LEYS, running invisibly over the whole surface of Earth, with certain topographical and astronomical factors. In Western history, the word geomancy was commonly used to describe a system of divination using the patterns created by pieces of soil cast on the ground. From China, the term FENG SHUI describes a successful and intact geomantic system which is becoming popular in the West today. Ultimately, geomancy has to do with the movement of spiritual energy throughout the Earth and between the Earth and this universe. This movement is basically calculated according to the harmonies of sacred geometry. The science of Earth energies: leys, DOWSING, grids, etc. Geomancy means "Earth measurement."

Germain, Comte de Saint. Said to have been born in 1561 and reincarnated many times, now an ascended Master. Historical research suggests he was, at different times, a European nobleman, an alchemist and mystic, and a leading spirit of the Rosicrucians, early advocates of the doctrines of theosophy and the development of psychic powers. The "I AM" Religious Movement begun by Guy Warren and Edna Ballard is a form of theosophy that envisions the ascended Masters known as the Great White BROTHERHOOD, particularly Saint Germain, as guiding the world toward a new, enlightened age. Biography by Isabel Cooper-Oakley: *The Comte de Saint Germain,* 1912.

Gestalt therapy. A didactic therapy in which we enact the role of self and other characters or symbols because they comprise the whole–the meaning of the German word *gestalt*. As a therapy, the movement of the mind that occurs as new insights are gained and breakthroughs in awareness realized.

Ghost. The nonphysical, or etheric, body of an entity that lingers in the dense world after death – especially when attracted.

Gifts of the Spirit. In 1 Corinthians 12.8-10 Paul named nine gifts of the spirit after Pentecost – the modern interpretation is included: 1) Wisdom – insight; 2) Knowledge – telepathy with divine mind, piercing the veil; 3) faith – inner knowing; 4) healing – of body, emotion, or mind; 5) working of miracles – use of laws beyond our understanding (psychokinesis/telekinesis); 6) prophecy – prophecy and dreams; 7) discerning of spirits – in spirit communication, discernment between astral and spiritual dimensions; 8) divers kinds of tongues – speaking from altered states; 9) interpretation of tongues – understanding what is channeled.

Glamour. Illusion on the astral plane intensified by desire. A false picture that, when held in the mind and charged with emotional energy, becomes a forceful and dominating factor, blinding and misleading us in order to secure satisfaction and survival. Groups and individuals create, maintain, and energize glamours, e.g., "Everyone who finishes college has it made." A glamour functions by arousing the emotional desire that produces or charges the false picture or belief. Through this process we eventually learn the lessons of life and dissolve the desires that hold us in bondage to personality.

Glyph. A character that demonstrates its meaning symbolically, as in ASTROLOGY, to symbolize the twelve signs of the zodiac and the planets.

Gnosis. The Greek word for "knowledge." Spiritual knowledge, especially the direct, immediate experience of the Divine that transcends cognitive reason. Rather than faith or good moral behavior, most Gnostics regarded this awareness as the way back to the true God. The mystical knowledge held in the CLOUD OF KNOWABLE THINGS and available to those who make themselves capable. Inner knowing by the power of intuition, the truth of the inner reality that guides us into harmony with the one great PLAN. Also called DAATH, SOPHIA.

Gnostic Gospels. Collections of truth teachings pertaining to a belief system. The Gnostics were persecuted and went into hiding in the early centuries of Christianity. All Gnostics were not Christians, but all were in touch with inner wisdom and belief in other realities.

Gnosticism. Any of a number of spiritual movements flourishing from the 1st to the 3rd centuries A.D. Though their tenets varied, most were radically dualistic, positing a good but alien God beyond the world of appearances and an inferior, usually malign God who has created this world. Gnostics–mystics who worked with inner revealed knowledge–considered *gnosis* to be the way back to the true God. The teachings of Gnosticism were declared heretical by the Roman church at the Council of Nicaea when the mystery tradition yielded to new forms of Christianity only to survive underground in hidden form. Some contemporary organizations and individuals holding either similar beliefs or embracing wisdom coming from mystical practices identify themselves as Gnostic.

Goal-fitness. An Agni term. The purpose that underlies all comeasurement and is the basis of cause and effect. Purpose particularly denotes Ray 1, the first aspect of Deity and thus the great ruling law of the universe. Each of us must have purpose to be sent forth and must fulfill that purpose to return. Thus goal-fitness acknowledges the purpose of each atom of creation.

God-Immanent. The God within creation. *See* Christ-within.

God-Transcendent. The God beyond the world of human affairs. The Supreme Intelligence that was from the beginning and is without end. The ultimate Source from which all life springs and to which all life returns.

God-within. The divine spark confined within matter which, in time, evolving DISCIPLES realize and honor with total allegiance.

Godhood. A name given by the Christ to the exalted state that created all life and beckons all humanity, reminding us, "Remember, ye are Gods." The state of divinity from which our creative nature is derived. "Made in the image and likeness"–it is our true nature as well.

Golden Age (of Harmony). An era, according to spiritual writings, when humanity awakens to its divine nature and demonstrates high consciousness. We read of Golden Ages of the past and of a promised and long-awaited age to emerge now in the Age of Aquarius. An age of peace, a time of harmony among all people and all kingdoms on Earth.

Golden cord. Biblical term for threads of the ANTAHKARANA that connect the soul to the body. *See* Aka cord.

Grace. An outpouring of spiritual power that frees from restriction and lifts the consciousness into a new state of awareness. We embrace love, freedom, beauty, and joy to invoke grace–a state gifted from the higher world when we realize a shift in consciousness that reveals the underlying and little-understood laws of life at work. Grace brings healing, freedom from restriction–perhaps physical, but not necessarily.

Granulation. An Agni term. Often used in connection to FOHAT to describe the earliest stirring and movement of primary matter, referring to a process far removed from the physical plane, as in the original "at the time of creation" when forms of energy-matter were beginning to differentiate.

Grapes. Bunches of grapes symbolize the wine of holy Communion. The grape vine or leaf is often used as an emblem of Jesus, the "true vine."

Great Advent. An Agni term. Helena Roerich used this term for the reappearance of the Christ, which she called the Great Individuality.

Great Cosmic Mother. The space that receives creation and holds the seeds of all potentialities, nurturing and sustaining life as it seeks expression.

Great Individuality, the. An Agni term. Helena Roerich used this term for the Christ in discussing the reappearance, which she called the GREAT ADVENT. Her comment is that the Great Lords take everything into consideration according to the Law of GOAL-FITNESS and that the world is not ready for the Great Individuality to return in physical form. She states the Great Individuality will rule – invisibly visible – equipped with the RAYS of the powerful but invisible LABORATORY.

Great Invocation, The. *See pages 74-75.*

Great Wholeness. A recognition of the Creator; a title for "About Whom Naught Can Be Said." Knowing we are all a part of the one body of Christ creates wholeness.

Group brothers. In esoteric thought, those with whom we find ourselves specifically linked in our spiritual growth. It is not sexist–it is used by male and female, convents and monasteries, somewhat like a "Class of 1998" or a number of people evolving together. The human and angelic kingdoms are brothers, as in "Am I my brother's keeper?"

Group meditation. "Where two or three are gathered in my name..." the power of the Christ is invoked and magnified.

Group mind. The blended consciousness of a number of associated people.

Group soul. The collection of unique qualities a group creates as it comes together to form a group action through an agreed-upon purpose or direction around a goal, a leader, or a central atom.

The Great Invocation

A mantra to be spoken by awakened ones. Given by the Master Djwhal Khul through Alice A. Bailey for the purpose of invoking Christ to come to the aid of suffering humanity. Three stanzas (1935, 1940, 1945) comprise the Great Invocation, but only the third is known widely and used by large numbers to create the "cry" of humanity for assistance to the human kingdom and the planet. Used with dedication by the WORLD SERVERS.

Stanza One (1935)
Let the Forces of Light
Bring illumination to mankind.
Let the Spirit of Peace be spread abroad.
May men of goodwill everywhere
Meet in a spirit of cooperation.
May forgiveness on the part of all men
Be the keynote at this time.
Let power attend the efforts of the Great Ones.
So let it be, and help us to do our part.

Stanza Two (1940)
Let the Lords of Liberation issue forth.
Let Them bring succour to the sons of men.
Let the Rider from the Secret Place come forth,
And coming, save.
Come forth, O Mighty One.

Let the souls of men awaken to the Light,
And may they stand with massed intent.
Let the fiat of the Lord go forth:
The end of woe has come!

Come forth, O Mighty One.
The hour of service of the Saving Force
Has now arrived.
Let it be spread abroad, O Mighty One.
Let Light and Love and Power and Death
fulfill the purpose of the Coming One.
The Will to save is here.
The Love to carry forth the work
Is widely spread abroad.
The Active Aid of all who know the truth
Is also here.

Stanza Three (1945)

From the point of Light within the Mind of God
Let light stream forth into the minds of men.
Let Light descend on Earth.

From the point of Love within the Heart of God
Let love stream forth into the hearts of men.
May Christ return to Earth.

From the center where the Will of God is known
Let purpose guide the little wills of men–
The purpose which the Masters know and serve.

From the center which we call the race of men
Let the Plan of Love and Light work out
And may it seal the door where evil dwells.

Let Light and Love and Power restore the Plan on Earth.

Guardian angel. A protective presence who may be summoned to strengthen our souls as we meet the challenges of human incarnation.

Guardian Band of the Planet. Hierarchy of the planetary Logos with an emphasis on the service it renders that guiding one, the Christ.

Guidance. Connecting with the inner self that provides a sense of knowing as we attune to a higher dimension of self. Until we connect with guidance from within, we need guidance from an outer mentor, a moral code, or ethical philosophy.

Guide. A discarnate spirit entity usually associated with communicating guidance, often thought to be a somewhat advanced friend in spirit with whom we have shared previous lives. A spirit friend who can provide some companionship in a new and spiritual realm.

Guided imagery. Visualizations and other uses of image-making mechanisms often guided by another for a purpose such as healing meditations or positive affirmations.

Guna. A Sanskrit term. The interactions of three electric qualities pervading all levels of creation responsible for the material universe. **Sattva,** the positive, dynamic influence, results in mental brightness and elevation. **Rajas,** the neutralizing influence of restlessness, is compulsive–activity for the sake of motion. **Tamas** is the negative influence of sluggishness and inertia. These forces are described, respectively, as action (will), rhythm (harmony), stability (inertia).

Guru. In Sanskrit *gu* means "darkness," and *ru* means "to illuminate." Combined, the word *guru* means "one who illumines the darkness." A spiritual teacher or guide; a master in metaphysical and ethical teachings who is identified with the grace of bestowing spiritual power on a disciple.

H

Habituation. The conditioning that results from repeated exposure.

Hall, Manly Palmer. b. Canada, 1901, d. 1990. Author, lecturer, and minister of an occult/metaphysical group in Los Angeles called The Church of the People. In 1934 he established the Philosophical Research Society, fulfilling a life-long dream of founding a school modeled on the ancient school of PYTHAGORAS to disseminate wisdom teachings throughout the West. *Reincarnation: The Cycle of Necessity*, 1939; *First Principles of Philosophy*, 1942; *Self-Unfoldment by Disciplines of Realization*, 1942; *The Mystical Christ*, 1951; *The Rosicrucians and Magister Cristoph Schlegel: Hermetic Roots of America*, 1986.

Halls of Learning. Three in number, each stands for a particular state of consciousness wherein we make contact with new awareness as we dissolve the veils that create the separate halls.

1) The Hall of Concentration is entered at the third initiation, or TRANSFIGURATION. Here we meet the ANGEL OF THE PRESENCE and receive great instructions and new understanding of the spiritual laws that guide life and each segment of creation.

2) In the Hall of Choice, related to the fourth initiation, initiates are prepared to stand on their own, between "the Earth and heaven," renounce all they have had and been, and withdraw from the physical side of life.

3) The Hall of Blinded Men is entered at the sixth or seventh initiation. The release of the veil of separation creates a tremendous light that blinds the initiates as they see the "glory of the Lord."

This concept is to help us understand that at each initiation we contact greater light, love, and synthesis for ourselves and for the human race in its quest for evolution. *See* Veils, four.

Harmlessness. Agni virtue for Sagittarius. Building a consciousness that can pass through the currents of the world without becoming destructive becomes the work. The Buddha in his time said, "It is not enough to cease to do evil, it is time to do good"; however, not all have yet built such a consciousness. Harmlessness not only does not set negatives into motion, but also creates a positive aura of protection about us. *See* Gandhi.

Harmonic Convergence. The initiating of the 25-year transition period, beginning in 1987, of leaving the Piscean Age and entering the Aquarian Age, according to the MAYA mysteries. These years have been divided into five-year segments comparable to the five stages of dying: 1987-1992, denial; 1992-1997, anger; 1997-2002, bargaining; 2002-2007, depression; 2007-2012, acceptance.

Harmony. Agni theme. Ugliness in all its aspects is a dangerous malady. For humanity's sake, we must understand its cure and where is its dissolution. It is time to understand that words should be beautiful and that harmony produces exalted thinking. We become the ones who learn to bring harmony to our words, colors, tones, and actions. Holding a place of peace within us, we expand this harmony to the world through will and love-wisdom. Correlates to the energy and influence of the number 6. *See* Numerology.

Hatha Yoga. *See* Yoga.

Healers, spiritual. Individuals using either the art or science of techniques of energy transference designed to recharge and/or balance the energy system of the etheric body in order to facilitate health and healing.

Healing rite. Anointing the sick and the dying with holy oil. The Christian rite–formerly known as the Last Rites of the Church–is felt to bring healing help to those in need, physical or spiritual. The deceased are anointed, and this acts as a closing of the chakras and the door between the planes. *See* Last Rites.

Heart. The heart is a symbol of God's love and the love of humans for one another. Its religious meaning can be found in 1 Samuel 16.7, "I do not see as man sees; for man looks on the outward appearance, but the Lord looks on the heart." The heart is also considered to be the source of understanding, love, courage, devotion, sorrow, and joy. The heart center (chakra) represents the positive emotional center of consciousness, the contact point of the mental nature to "thinketh in the heart."

An Agni word referring to the purified heart, the accumulator that permits passage of the manifestation of the subtle FOHAT, the light of a special quality to emanate into expression. Heart is often used to mean soul or soul quality.

Heaven and hell. Two designated points of experiences in the astral reality. Heaven denotes higher, more beauty-filled levels; hell (or hades) denotes the pain-filled realms.

Heindel, Max. b. Carl Louis Van Grasshof, Germany, 1865, d. 1919. Student of Rudolf Steiner and founder of the Rosicrucian Fellowship. In 1907 an elder brother of the ancient Rosicrucian Order appeared to him and transmitted the material eventually published as the *Rosicrucian Cosmo-Conception.* His work with the ephemeris, tables showing the daily positions of the planets, led to a new and widespread interest in astrology. *The Rosicrucian Mysteries,* 1911; *Message of the Stars,* 1913; *Sim-*

plified Scientific Astrology, 1928, *Rosicrucian Philosophy in Questions and Answers,* 1922.

Heline, Corinne. b. Georgia, 1882, d. 1975. Author, musician, and healer. A student of Max Heindel, founder of the Rosicrucian Fellowship, in 1922 she received what was called an "inner commission" to interpret the Bible in the esoteric tradition, which was to become a life-long work. The New Age Bible and Philosophy Center in California was established in the 1930s to disseminate her many works. She married Theodore Heline in 1938 and the New Age Press was established. *New Age Bible Interpretation* (in seven volumes), including *Mystery of the Christos,* 1961; *The Cosmic Harp,* 1969; *Color and Music in the New Age,* 1964; *Healing and Regeneration through Colors,* 1943.

Heraclitus. c. 500 B.C. Greek philosopher whose most famous doctrine is that everything is in a state of flux–you can never step into the same river twice. What appears to be a changeless stability of the world conceals a dynamic tension between opposites which is controlled by reason (logos) or its physical manifestation, fire; and that fire is the ultimate constituent of the world. The fire of the human

79

soul is thus connected to the cosmic fire which virtuous souls will eventually join. *On Nature, Fragments.*

Heretic. By derivation, "one who is able to choose." Thus, all who choose to think for themselves, rather than believe what they are told, are heretics. They have a noble predecessor in St. Paul who, in his first epistle to the Thessalonians (5.20-21), counseled, "Do not reject prophecies. Prove all things, uphold that which is good."

Hermes Trismegistus. "The Thrice Great." The Greek Scribe of the Gods, God of Wisdom, and the Egyptian God Thoth. A legendary Egyptian sage, said to be the author of the Tarot, Neo-Platonism, the Kabalah, alchemy, and astrology. He gave rise to Hermetism, a school of mystical religious thought of significant influence in the Middle Ages and the Renaissance. Based on "The Hermetics," a series of philosophical treatises written by various authors between the 2nd and 4th centuries A.D., the tracts include astrological writings from the Egyptian tradition, Persian secret rites, and interest in regenerative experience and religious ecstasy from Greek sources.

Hermetic chain. The hidden influence that creates the "Ladder of Life," or the evolutionary chain, hard at work, pushing consciousness forward. Out of sight, this force brings opportunities to learn and grow, to satisfy unfinished business, and to provide challenges to overcome.

Hermetic tradition. The closely held, hidden traditions of wisdom teachings, usually given an aspirant or disciple under strict circumstances and instruction by a guru or mentor; not necessarily religious in nature.

Hexagram. A six-pointed star formed by extending each of the sides of a regular hexagram (six sides) into equilateral triangles. As two interlocking triangles, the  hexagram symbolizes "as above so below." This configuration begins as two triangles touch–one descending Earthward, the other pointing upward. The first represents the soul reaching downward and the second is personality reformed and ready. As they touch, they represent the lower three chakras ready and the top three chakras stirring. When the heart

Hermetic Principles. Seven in number, considered the underlying foundation for life in the material world. *See individual definitions;* Universal law.

1. Mentalism	All is mind; creative intelligence flows from divine mind.
2. Correspondence	As above, so below; know thyself, if you would know another.
3. Vibration	Everything is in motion; physics has proven higher vibrations are merely purer matter.
4. Polarity	Everything is reflected by opposites; poles of duality form a line of tension that keeps each extreme related and reflective.
5. Rhythm	Everything flows in and out; the pendulum swings; rhythm compensates.
6. Cause and Effect	Every action has a related action, or nothing happens without a reason. *Karma* is the Sanskrit word of the law of relationship between first cause and outcome.
7. Gender	All things are masculine and feminine energies at work, expressing as generation, regeneration, creation. To be pure, we respect gender; disrespect moves us to self-destruction.

(the fourth chakra) opens, the triangles blend into the disciple, the six-pointed star.

Hierarchy. The delegated, directive supreme authority and power overseeing planetary life on the higher planes, guiding and teaching initiates and disciples. Also known as the Great White Brotherhood or orders/brotherhoods of initiated souls working as a field of intelligence serving the Creator. Holy ones who demonstrate leadership and service, awakening humanity to its greater potential and revealing a path of ascent to higher realities of life for those aware of Hierarchy. Consisting of many departments, different qualifications, branches of the Plan, this inner structure holds the blueprint for humanity as, one by one, personalities come to know themselves as one great soul, the human soul incarnated in the world of matter. *See* Brotherhood.

Hierarchy of a constellation. The sacred line of power bequeathed by a constellation to affect lesser life in its process of evolution. *See* Celestial hierarchies.

Hierarchy, planetary. *Hier* means "sacred" and *archy* means "to rule." Over-seeing planetary life on the higher planes, this delegated, supreme authority directs, guides, and teaches initiates and disciples. Also known as the Great White BROTHERHOOD, these orders or groups of initiated souls work as a field of intelligence serving the Creator, or the Plan of Creation. The sacred line of power that guides all life within a planetary scheme to its particular goal according to a higher Plan. The group of spiritual beings existing on the inner planes of the solar system which is the intelligent and directive force responsible for the evolutionary processes of the Earth. Additionally, advanced ones of twelve CELESTIAL HIERARCHIES influence planetary energies for the benefit of all life. Hierarchy is reflected in the Earth scheme–described by the OCCULTIST as "the occult Hierarchy formed of CHOHANS, ADEPTS, and INITIATES working through their DISCIPLES and, by this means, in the world."

Hierophant. The initiator who stands as a representative of the HIERARCHY within the more subtle plane or on Earth. In the inner world the great initiator is the Christ. "No one comes unto the Father except by me," for he is the teacher of angels and of humanity for this planet. On the Earth the person who is chosen by the inner world and who serves by GNOSIS is the real initiator. Many copies are GLAMOURS and invalid as far as spiritual worth is concerned.

High consciousness. An expanded state of knowing or understanding characterized by increased awareness and sensitivity to seen and unseen realities. Also, the practice of an ethical lifestyle guided by high principles. The consciousness achieved through activation of the higher chakras.

High self. The ball of wisdom, or sum total of awareness, an evolving soul gleans through personal experiences in this and all previous incarnations. This ball of knowledge serves as a high point in consciousness, guiding personality as it experiences life within the limited awareness of physical form.

Higher and lower minds. The two departments of the mental body that vibrate to the personality and to the soul. The midpoint (fourth level of seven) is a place of decisive development and the home of the High Self and the Christ-potential within humanity.

Higher third. A specific technique that comes from Eastern thought designed to lessen the sense of loss experienced in compromise. When two opposing points are to be reconciled, each point seeks to lift perspective and move closer to the other, forming a triangle of movement–higher and toward center–until a point of reconciliation is found. The technique is called the Law of Higher Third.

 Higher triad. In a sequence of triangles, the highest. Example: chakras one, two, and three create a lower, or physical, triad; three, four, and five create the psychological triad, and five, six, and seven create a higher, or spiritual, triad. The kabalistic TREE OF LIFE depicts three triads, as do many other systems. The triangle composed of the subtlest energies is, of course, the highest of the three triangles.

Hinduism. An Eastern religion of antiquity that gave birth to Buddhism–similar to Judaism generating Christianity. The religion of Brahma, Vishnu, and Shiva. Krishna was considered an incarnation of Vishnu; Babaji of Herakhan is considered an incarnation of Shiva.

Ho. The Native American word for affirming "and so it is" or "I agree." A power word when used as a mantra.

Hod. This eighth sephirah on the kabalistic Tree of Life is called "splendor" (specifically the splendor of the mind).

Holism. A term used for the aspects of self-synthesizing. The holism of self leads to whole, wholesome, and holy.

Holistic. A term affirming the nature of all to be whole–at one, a synthesis of many parts–establishing a greater state when all is unified.

Holy Ghost. In the Christian tradition, a similar term to the Holy Spirit. The etheric imprint held in each level of ethers; the clear reflective ether holds the blueprint, and other levels hold the consciousness that expresses through personality. This forms the shadow side of the divine–God in matter–and will exist until all is drawn back into rest.

Holy Grail, the. The archetype for the chalice into which higher awareness can flow, and a symbol of the process necessary to gain holy consciousness.

Holy Orders. A public vow of life of service to God and to the work of Spirit. A conscious commitment of allegiance with the forces of Light in the work within and for humanity regarding enlightenment (salvation). Responding to the call of the Soul to live not for ourselves alone, but for others and for God. Taking a public vow to serve and to stand for our spiritual beliefs. This may be monastic, as a nun or monk, a priest, a minister–lay or ordained.

Holy Spirit. The third person of the Trinity; the power of active intelligence in the universe. An aspect of divine consciousness that expresses in the physical realm without physical form through overshadowing those who are receptive as souls to this high frequency or intelligence. The aspect of divine nature that is the vital, form-building energy ensouling all matter. Generally considered to be feminine. The divine-within that delivers creative

expression from the world of spirit to the world of form–the MAHAT. Also known as Christ-Consciousness, the Comforter, SOPHIA, Holy Breath, and Holy Ghost.

Holy week. The seven days of the Christian tradition between Palm Sunday and Easter Sunday designating the fire mysteries, depicted in the crucifixion and resurrection rites.

Hope of glory. Divine potential awaiting expression.

House. An astrological chart is divided into twelve sections creating a wheel. These sections, or houses, are each approximately 30 degrees and signify the relative division of the heavens according to the birthplace and the birth time of an individual or event. Each house represents a basic field of activity or experience, the meaning of which is modified by the planets occupying the house and the sign that rules the house due to its placement on the house cusp.

Human group mind. In esoteric teachings the mind of the whole of humanity–both incarnate and discarnate; a synthesis of human consciousness. Humanity's shared AKASHIC RECORD, as per Eastern symbology, where all universal knowledge is held – past, present, and future. Correlates to the collective unconscious of humanity.

Humanitarian love. Latin: *humanus.* The bonds of affection that move a person to nurture and embrace another simply because each is a member of the human family and understands the inherent kinship and unity of all people. Devoted to the welfare of human beings; philanthropic.

Humanity. Agni theme. We learn to identify as one with humanity, knowing the work we do is for the well-being of the whole human race–the lifting of group consciousness. As we each make sacred our own nature, burning away the distortions, we realize our bond with all of humanity, and compassion results. Correlates to the energy and influence of the number 2.

Humility. Agni virtue for Aquarius. Humility is never an aspect of denigrating ourselves; that would distort the great truth of our being. Humility is surrendering the nonself to the High Self or acquiescing the personality to that which is our true purpose.

Huna. A Polynesian/Hermetic tradition focused on wholeness with an understanding of how each aspect contributes to the whole. A complex and well-developed science of health and ethical living practiced in the Pacific Islands.

Hunab K'U. The Maya solar deity, Creator of Measure and Movement.

Hypnotism. An altered state of consciousness wherein the individual, in a sleep-like condition, is quite responsive to suggestions made by the hypnotist.

I

I-Am presence (or consciousness). Derived from the mantra "I am that I am." An affirmation of our identity with the divine presence that brings about enlightenment and spiritual empowerment. Used in the practice of meditation and contemplation to affirm the indwelling and divine Self. An identification with all that is, with the one God who is within and who animates all things.

"I am that I am." A meditation SEED THOUGHT excellent for exploring. Our true nature is the relationship of the Self-within to the Self, the whole. Using this phrase as a seed thought assists us in knowing our genuine essence and uniting us in the oneness of the universe. We each learn we are a reflecting creation of the Great I Am.

"I Am the Soul." A phrase that is used much like an affirmation to remind our nonself of our true identity. We neutralize the belief that we are a person with a soul, and instead come to know we are a soul having a human experience. "I Am the Soul" is the true reality, and we are constantly seeking to realize it more deeply.

I Ching. *The Book of Changes.* An ancient Chinese book of wisdom and philosophy composed of sixty-four sections called hexagrams. Historically used as a source or tool of divination in conjunction with the tossing of coins or yarrow stalks. The text, beautifully composed, gives spiritual direction emphasizing ethical living and right-relationships, as understood through the observance of nature and the cycles of the heavens and Earth.

Ichthus. This earliest symbol for Christ, *ichthus,* is the Greek word for "fish." The five Greek letters spelling fish, *IXOYS,* form an anagram for the name and title of Christ: Jesus Christ, Son of God, Savior. Christianity was an underground movement for its first three hundred years. The ichthus gave the first Christians a secret sign by which followers could identify themselves as believers while it remained a mere decoration to outsiders. For this reason it was frequently used in early Christian art and literature. It appears many times in the catacombs of Rome, sometimes alone, sometimes in fishing scenes and in themes from the holy Eucharist.

Ida. One part of a threefold thread or channel in the spinal column. This channel is in the subtle body and is traversed by means of spiritual practices and disciplines under the guidance of a Master or teacher. The current on the left is called Ida or Ira and is associated with the feminine flow- or form-side of the currents of the KUNDALINI.

"If therefore the eye be single, the whole body shall be filled with light." Matthew 6.22 (KJV) refers to the single focus of mind and soul to be as one in order to guide us in the living of life. Generally accepted as referring to the spiritual "eye" being opened. Also called the "third eye," "eye center," or "brow chakra." The Peshitta Bible reads "the eye be bright," meaning "filled with radiance."

IHS. The letters IHCOYC are the name of Jesus in Greek. As Latin became the dominant language in the years following Jesus' death, the Greek "C" of IHCOYC was changed to a Latin "S." Thus the abbreviation became IHS instead of IHC. In ancient times, there was a widespread use of this monogram of Christ. It is most often incorporated in a Latin cross form.

Illumination. As light (perception, understanding, and realization) ignites the mind, concepts are comprehended, and the mysteries of life stand revealed. "The light puts out darkness."

Illusions. Distortions of the mental nature that masquerade as truth and claim our allegiance until we encounter an equally strong, differing perspective. Illusions stand as guideposts of false concepts to direct us in ever-widening spirals until they are confronted. Less emotionally charged than glamours, they are more dangerous because, more subtle because common, they are accepted as "truth": "My way is the only way." Clearing illusions is a great work for those on the path of initiation: false interpretations; mirages that exist individually and collectively for humanity ultimately to clear. In occultism everything finite (such as the universe and all in it) is "illusion," or "maya." It is one of the original definitions for "sin." A living thoughtform maintained and energized by personal or group belief. To awaken from illusion, we have to learn something that changes our mental concept or causes dis-illusions. Every illusion is a hindrance to freedom. Before we can function on higher levels of the mental plane or enter into the freedom of the intuitional plane, we must clear ourselves of illusions through meditation and will. This cleansing process often causes pain in the personal life.

Imagination. The vital ability of the mind to create and hold images for a variety of reasons: to etch into place desired programming to use in manifestation or to reflect symbols and pictures from either personality-level awareness or soul impressions. This delicate mechanism is of significant importance to move impressions from higher levels to levels of mind vibrating more slowly in order to manifest.

Image-making mechanism. A level of mind wherein the ability to image is developed, commonly referred to as "imagination." An important step in evolution is achieved when we can visualize, i.e., use the image-making mechanism.

Immaturity. This barrier to spiritual growth is acknowledged when we realize we respond from personality rather than from the soul maturity our nature has to offer. Once noted, guidelines can be given to assist the maturing process. Use of love and will, objectivity, developing the perspectives of other aspects of our nature all help the process. Freedom from the selfish ego identity is a major work in the maturing process.

Immorality. Practices inconsistent with the ethics of a moral life.

Immortality. Without cease; eternal. Life that cannot end but continues beyond the demise of the physical.

Imperil. An Agni term. A crystalline precipitate within the nerve channels of an organism, formed in response to an irritant or negative form of stimulation. Highly toxic to the organism, it is the most contaminating ingredient of the human condition. It can be dissolved only by high-level, opposing frequencies of truth, beauty, and goodness, together with complete rest.

Imprint. The pattern that lingers in the mind after contact with soul energy or awareness.

Incense. A sweet smelling preparation used to clean the astral level of a given area. Often used to clear and cleanse a space dedicated to spiritual work to aid in invoking spiritual power or holy influences. Incense can be burned to help neutralize negative energies or to clear the space of unhealthy influences.

Inclusiveness. Movement away from fragmentation and toward embracing all facets or aspects of ourselves or of the greater Oneness.

Individuation. The journey of consciousness as it departs from tribal awareness to proceed to a point of singular mental identity (the ego) which will become an integrated personality. Individuation assists us toward the greater experience of Oneness as egos evolve into higher consciousness.

Inertia. This barrier to spiritual growth arises from the lowest GUNA. The tendency to not advance, laziness, satisfaction with status quo, dullness.

Initiates. From Latin root meaning "first principles of any science." Those dedicated to the study and mastery of the mysteries of the science of self, the One Self in all selves. Those who have made themselves ready to enter upon the Path of Initiation, culmination of the path of human evolution–in most Western systems divided into five steps called "initiations." In the esoteric Christian path, these steps are modeled by the life of Jesus, THE CHRIST. Before the first initiation, we are "aspirants" or "candidates" and on the probationary path. Common terms are "disciple" for second degree, "initiate" for third degree.

Initiation. A process of awakening to our true identity and using it in service to humanity; admission into sacred teachings or the spiritual life; the process of understanding or expansion of consciousness. Also, admission into the sacred teachings or organizations of an esoteric or occult discipline.

Initiation, the Path of. The modern journey of esoteric Christianity contains seven major events.
  1. The birth of the Christ-within
  2. Baptism
  3. Transfiguration
  4. Crucifixion
  5. Revelation
  6. Decision
  7. Resurrection
The first five are taken in connec-

tion with humanity, the last two usually not.

Inner alignment. The establishment of right-working relationship between levels of consciousness and levels of being, especially as the term is used to create an awareness of inner resources in order to know our inner nature.

Inner child. The modern term for the level of inner self imprinted by energies and experiences of our formative years, as well as programmed unconsciously. *See* Child-within.

Inner knower. The wise level of self that remains connected to the ball of knowledge or soul awareness that can be invited into present life situations.

Inner planes. Higher or hidden frequencies of each plane not recognized while conscious in the physical, awakened state, i.e., an inner-plane experience refers to an event occurring out of sight, most often behind the veil of sleep – revealed in a somewhat dreamlike manner but not a product of the subconscious; neither is it a dream, but an experience of another dimension imprinted on the memory in a delicate, gossamer awareness.

Inner planes classes. Gatherings behind the veil of sleep to which aspirants can be called during sleep and out-of-body to assist and hasten evolution of consciousness. Also called HALLS OF LEARNING, where ideas and concepts are introduced, or CHAPELS OF SILENCE, where energies, forces, or influences are rendered. Gatherings are called "classes," regardless of the type of exposure that takes place.

Inner presence. A point of consciousness at which we become aware–in an altered state that differs from the personality of the experiencer.

Inner reality. A different reality rules the spiritual nature than rules the personality. As we comprehend this, the task becomes to "know thyself" and then to bring the outer into alignment with the inner.

Inner self. The spiritual nature, often hidden even from ourselves.

Inner worlds. A realm of realities not recognized by the analytical, outer mental state.

INRI. An abbreviation using the four initials of the Latin inscription nailed above Jesus's head at the crucifixion, INRI stands for *Jesus Nazarenus Rex Judaeorum,* which means "Jesus of Nazareth, King of the Jews."

Instinctual mind. The intelligence that abides beneath the surface of intellect and that governs our body with its survival senses.

Instinctual thinking. The unconscious mental process that creates form.

Integral Yoga. *See* Yoga.

Intentional community. A group of individuals united around an intent or vision with a specific purpose or reason for being.

Inter-solar group. Inter-cosmic forces helping the evolution of planetary Logos, playing a role in balancing advancement toward the goal of the greater whole.

Intuition. A wisdom of the heart. Direct or spiritual perception, a subjective sense belonging to the soul. Spiritual intellect; insight by the intellect of the soul from the mind of Reality itself, beyond the domain of pure reason. A knowing or awareness at a level of mind or consciousness beyond mental reasoning or normal intellectual comprehension.

Intuitive consciousness. The level of mind also known as Christ consciousness or Buddhic consciousness, that plane of soul awareness which seeks to penetrate the mental nature so its impress can be recorded and recognized.

Invisible worlds. Realities more subtle than the physical senses can detect, therefore, not visible to the physical eye but detectable by other than physical senses.

Invocation. A prayer or statement used to call forth assistance from a higher power.

Invoke. To petition for support; to call forth through prayer, incantation, concentration, projection, or visualization, e.g., "Lord, heal my son." To request assistance of higher forces to act upon the lower worlds. A manner of summoning power, influence, or action from an unseen force, level, or source. To petition a desired power or energy to influence the physical world in a specific manner.

Involution (period of). A stage or process in which spirit or life descends into matter called "path of descent." Involution of spirit into matter happens so that form may be built, enabling evolution. Often referred to as the "fall," this is the result of souls wanting to know the secrets of life.

Involutionary period (human). The stage of the descent of spirit into matter characterized by the development and specialization of the form side of human life. The processes through which the senses are developed and the apparatus is perfected by the Self for the utilization of matter. A model that describes this process is the concept of the MONAD from which flows a stream of energy into denser physical planes. This monadic current–which, as a spark of God, is immortal and One with the Absolute–forms a point of consciousness called the Soul which in turn projects a part of itself to form a personality in the physical world. The projection of the monad–the soul in human form–is unconscious on this plane and expresses through personality to gain experience and awareness. In time it can develop a creator consciousness in the dense world and reunite with the original Source through the process of evolution.

Involution is the descent
of spirit into matter;
evolution is the
matter-to-spirit return.

Involutionary period (planetary). A stage or process preceding evolution in which spirit or life descends into matter–also called the "path of descent." Involution of spirit into matter happens so that form may be built, making possible its evolution. Descent into matter

is typically represented by a series of planets in which the least physical form is a mental globe (a thoughtform in the mind of God); then an astral form (made of the feeling or reflective ethers); then an etheric model firmer than the previous forms; and lastly the physical model which vibrates as matter and is the most densely concentrated form.

Iridology. The science of the study of the iris of the eye. This diagnostic system "reads" current and past health conditions by the appearance of the physical eyes.

Ishvara. The center point equivalent to the cosmic spirit within our being; the moment manifestation begins, "a point" of manifestation, as though held in the bosom of God. Also, the name of the family home where NICHOLAS ROERICH lived as a child in Russia, about one hundred miles from St. Petersburg.

Isis. Egyptian deity, personification of the divine Mother.

Islam. A world religion established by Mohammed approximately seven hundred years after the life of Jesus and the beginning of Christianity. A Ray 6 religion of great passion and devotion. Islam considers Mecca its holy city and Jesus a great prophet. It claims a relationship to both Judaism and Christianity and is the fastest growing religion in the world today. *Islam* means "submission" (to God). A principal emphasis of Islam is how to live a holy life, with strict rules for daily life, as presented in its holy book, the Koran.

J

Jacob's ladder. In KABALAH, the overlay of the four worlds from the densest to the least dense when the appropriate sephiroth overlay each other, thereby creating a stairway from the lowest point (Malkuth on Assiah) to the highest (Kether in Atziluth). Also, in the Old Testament, Jacob's dream experience when he saw the angels descending and ascending the planes of creation, between heaven and Earth. (Gen. 28.12) The esoteric implication is that each soul descended into matter to learn and experience. Now we must build a point of consciousness on each plane, level by level, and then express that awareness in order to return to the higher reality.

Jesus. Master of Ray 6 (devotion) and wayshower of the Christian religion. The life of Master Jesus is used as the example for the human path of initiation in Esoteric Christianity. *See* Christ, historical.

Jesus prayer. "Lord Jesus Christ, Son of God, have mercy on me."

Jewel in the Lotus. A name given in Eastern spiritual traditions to the soul as that point of consciousness that steps down the energies of the MONAD to the personality and acts as a guiding light. Also referred to as the True Self, the I-Am Presence, the highest aspect of monadic manifestation, the central nucleus or inner flame, the focal point of energy in the SPIRITUAL TRIAD, or the liberated Self who is attuned to God- or Creator-Consciousness.

Jnana Yoga. *See* Yoga.

Journaling. Recording thoughts freely expressed in the privacy of our writing; open sharing on paper of thoughts and impressions. Frequently the free-flow triggers latent knowledge and thoughts to be lifted into recognition by the conscious mind. May precipitate an opening awareness or experience from the right hemisphere of the brain.

Joy. Agni virtue for Pisces. First we must discern the difference between happiness and joy. Happiness fluctuates by the actions of the outer world; joy is that which sustains us while the happiness rises and falls. Joy touches the energy of the soul–a charge that floods us like SAMADHI, the peace that passes understanding.

Judaism. The Hebrew religion of the Jewish people. A Ray 5 religion with strict rules for spiritual living, considered the religion of the Aries Age and the tree from which Christianity arose. Master Jesus, the Great Initiate and Wayshower of Christianity, was a recognized wise one of Judaism.

Jung, Carl Gustav. b. Switzerland, 1875, d. 1961. Psychiatrist and collaborator with Sigmund Freud until their parting over differences concerning the role of sexuality in neuroses. From his research into fantasies and dreams, he affirmed that these arise from the collective unconscious, a "reservoir of memories in each person that precedes historical memory." He saw the archetype as an instinctive pattern, a basic universal image in the dream life of people of many unrelated cultures, and dream symbols as indications of religious intuition and revelation. He found among many religious traditions the symbols of quaternity, trinity, and duality. The animus-anima or male-female components together, he believed, expressed the interaction and wholeness that belong to being human. He saw the MANDALA as an archetypal image of the psyche, a symbolic expression of the soul's feeling of total completeness–unity with nature, unity with humanity, and unity with God. He thought the goal of psychic development to be the Self. *Psychic Energy*, 1928; *Psychology and Religion*, 1937; *The Undiscovered Self*, 1957; Autobiography: *Memories, Dreams, Reflections*, 1962; *Man and His Symbols*, 1964.

K

Kabalah (also Kabbala, Kabbalah, Cabala, Qabbalah, et al.) The occult philosophy of Judaism based on  an esoteric interpretation of the Hebrew scriptures and passed down as a secret doctrine to the initiated. Regarded as essential in most schools of occultism, the Kabalah is the "spirit" of Judaism – its mystical part as opposed to the "letter" of its law. This hidden wisdom, or theosophy, of the Jewish religion – basically the unity of God and creation – purportedly had its basis in the archaic Chaldean secret doctrine and was obtained by the rabbis of the Middle Ages from precepts concerning divine truth and cosmogony. The word itself was derived from the Hebrew root, QBL, meaning "to receive," and refers to the practice of relaying esoteric knowledge by word of mouth. By some accounts, this system of theosophy is of celestial origin and was given to early Hebrew patriarchs through the ministry of angels. King David and King Solomon are said to have been initiated into the Kabalah and Rabbi Simeon Ben Jochai was to have written down a portion of these mystical teachings at the time of the destruction of the second temple. His son, Rabbi Eleazar, his secretary, and his disciples gathered his treatises and from them composed the Zohar, meaning "splendor," which is the literary source of kabalism.

Kabalists. Those who study and practice the Hebrew mystery teachings, the Kabalah, and interpret the hidden meaning of the scriptures.

Kahunas. The priests and priestesses of the Huna tradition – literally "keepers of the secret." Originally from Hawaii and the South Pacific, Max Freedom Long studied, observed, and wrote as his lifetime effort five volumes, the classic texts on the Huna tradition, its philosophy, ideology, and healing concepts.

Kali-Yuga. In Eastern teachings, the period of destruction and planetary purification now in progress and from which our world is emerging. *Kali* means "iron" and reminds us of the many challenges the Industrial Age will present for those who follow.

Kama. Emotion, desire.

Kama manas. Mind colored by desire (ambition/personal love, masculine/feminine–equally selfish). The lower mind or animal soul for lower or reincarnating ego.

Karma. Literally, action, deed, or work. The total of all of our actions, both presently and in previous lives. Also, the law of ethical causation, or cause and effect, the spiritual law wherein we eventually experience the consequences of all of our actions – positive and negative. This universal law insures justice for each soul as it experiences creation. As consciousness evolves, karma requires adjustment and/or compensation for all "pluses" and "minuses"–individual, group, and planetary. Not good, not bad; just "just."

Karma-free action. Opportunities to express ignorance without penalty, usually in response to a command or instruction given from a being of higher comprehension; we earn merit for obedience even if actions are not wise.

Karma, Law of. Also known as the law of cause and effect. One of seven ever-just universal laws that guide all life in its evolving consciousness: the HERMETIC PRINCIPLES, or Hermetic Laws, of 1) Mentalism, 2) Correspondence, 3) Vibration, 4) Polarity, 5) Rhythm, 6) Cause and Effect, 7) Gender. These collective influences maintain and support life through its processes of creation, orderliness, and destruction. Within the framework of this structure, numerous operations of cause and effect are defined.

Karma Yoga. *See* Yoga.

Karmic debt. That which is due as a result of previous action(s). Cause initiates effect and is as related as two sides of a coin.

Karmic sheet. The record of cause and effect already in place.

Kestrel. This small falcon, also known as the sparrow hawk, was revered by the ancient Egyptians for its ability to fly vertically as well as horizontally, symbolizing the ascension of spirit in esoteric teachings.

Kether. The highest-vibrating (first) sephirah on the TREE OF LIFE in Kabalah, equated with the crown chakra, the highest of all energy centers in each of the four worlds of the Kabalah.

This center is also known as SHAMBALLA in Agni Yoga and as "highest heaven" in Christianity.

Keynote. A sentence or statement providing an underlying theme, tone, or focus. When used as a seed thought, the keynote establishes a vibration or tone to magnetize additional thoughts and insights to itself. It may refer to a thought used during a full Moon period or relating to a specific goal or occasion. The keynote of the lunar cycle focuses more tightly upon transitory energies than the seed thought in order to concentrate the Sun-Moon impact of the period. Also, our fundamental response to life, determined by Ray and sub-ray. This inner tone magnetizes a quality and style, our strengths and weaknesses by its fundamental presence, and then strives to overcome the limitations imposed through this collection.

Keys. As a religious symbol, keys often represent the keys to heaven as given to Peter. A housekey may admit or exclude a person. As a psychic symbol, a key, or tool, is being presented to capture our attention.

K'in. The Mayan word for "light," a power word when spoken as a mantra.

Kinesiology. A technique using touch to determine information stored at a subtle level beneath the awareness of the rational mind.

Kinesthetic. Relating to the sense of touch, i.e., acknowledging information gained through the sense of touch.

Kingdom of Souls. More modern terminology for the Kingdom of God, as used in the New Testament. The manifestation of a new kingdom of soul-conscious beings who are to emerge by evolution of the human king-dom into a new group mind – similar to the manner in which the human kingdom came forth from the animal kingdom to establish its own evolutionary reason for being.

Kirlian photography. A technique of measuring the emanations of life force radiated by any physical or etheric body. Developed by Semyon and Valentina Kirlian in Russia in 1939, it was first reported in this country by Sheila Ostrander and Lynn Schroeder in their book, *Psychic Discoveries Behind the Iron Curtain.*

"Know thyself." An ancient injunction inscribed over the temple of Apollo at Delphi. The teachings held that to know another, we must first know ourselves.

Knower. The impersonal level of awareness created through objectivity and spiritual insight that – as it is saturated by the awareness of the Soul – becomes increasingly active with aspects of soul insight to help the integrated personality in the living of life.

Koans. Contemplative thoughts in the Zen school of wisdom. Paradoxes.

Koran. The sacred book of scriptures of the Islamic religion.

Krishna. A Hindu deity, considered an incarnation of Vishnu,

the most celebrated avatar. The reputed speaker and teacher in the *Bhagavad Gita.* Krishna is India's greatest prophet. His teachings have many similarities to those of Jesus. To Westerners he is often regarded as an incarnation of the Christ.

Krishna Yoga. *See* Yoga.

Krishnamurti, Jiddu. b. So. India, 1895, d. 1986. Perceived by Charles Leadbeater and the Theosophical Society as the new world teacher. As a young man, he was prepared for the role of Maitreya by Annie Besant, president of the Theosophical Society; however, he renounced the assigned role and pursued his own way as author and teacher. Krishnamurti maintained that organized beliefs are "an impediment to inner liberation." *The World of Peace,* 1985.

Kriya Yoga. *See* Yoga.

Kriyashakti. A Sanskrit term. "Made in the image and likeness of God." Creative power used in forming all creation.

Kuan Yin. The Eastern name given to the Chinese feminine deity which appears from time to time to inspire and comfort humanity, known as the BODHI-SATTVA OF COMPASSION. She is the embodiment of beauty and purity. As the wise woman of matriarchy, the healer-teacher sage, she represents the three aspects of holding strength in restraint, unity, and caring love.

Kumaras. Guardians of the power of planets; arbiters of nations and continents; judges of good and evil.

Kundalini. The primal energy of the universe, some part of which lies coiled in potential form at the base of the human spine. When channeled upward through the body to the brain, it is associated with the state of enlightenment. As this powerful spiritual energy awakens from dormancy, it rises along the spine activating the chakras, igniting change, stimulating life activity. The awakening of this mystical force is related closely to the process of spiritual evolution which leads toward final union with the divine, or God-realization.

Kundalini Yoga. *See* Yoga.

Kurukshetra. The battleground, burning ground, a point of friction between personality and spirit for transmuting forces and forging new awareness. A second major stage occurs as the ARHAT completes burning ties to the human condition.

L

Laboratory. An Agni term. A reference to the planes and worlds of creation wherein lessons, expansion of consciousness, learning, and growing are always occurring.

Labyrinth. An intricate single-path design of a specific number of circuits from the outside to the cen-ter; not a maze, which may have dead-ends or false turns. The classic design calls for seven circuits. At the center of this "invisible temple" is the heart (or goal, or womb, or Sun). An excellent tool as a walking meditation for physical, emotional, mental, and spiritual harmony and balance. Often constructed over LEYS. Circuits can be associated with the CHAKRA system or the ZODIAC.

Lama. The title given to monks of a sect of BUDDHISM originating in the Tibetan, or Mongolian, part of the world.

Lao-Tzu. 6th century B.C. Chinese philosopher, mystic, and sage who is regarded as the inspiration of Taoism. Lao-Tzu taught how to keep apart from the world, yet to remake it by following, Tao, the Way–the Way of evolution, of life, of reason, of the cosmos. The *Tao Te Ching,* the "Book of the Way and of Virtue" and the "bible" of Taoism, seems to presage the Christian Gospels with admonitions to "Repay evil with good," and, "Walk in the Way and you shall find peace." Marcus Bach: *Major Religions of the World,* 1959.

Last rites. Usually thought of in connection with death, last rites are truly an invoking of life force for

Labours of Hercules. From Greek mythology. A path of discipleship is depicted through Hercules' labours as he astrologically enacted the life history of every aspirant. *Herculas* means "the incarnated, not-yet perfect Son of God." Hercules was a son of humanity and of God. The twelve labours are archetypes of zodiacal influences depicted as duties Hercules must perform:

Aries, the capture of the man-eating mares
Taurus, the capture of the Cretan bull
Gemini, gathering the golden apples of the Hesperides
Cancer, capture of the doe or hind
Leo, the slaying of the Nemean lion
Virgo, seizing the girdle of Hippolyte
Libra, the capture of the Erymanthian boar
Scorpio, destroying the Lernaean hydra
Sagittarius, killing the Styphalian birds
Capricorn, the slaying of Cerberus, guardian of Hades
Aquarius, cleansing the Augean stables
Pisces, the capture of the red cattle of Geryon

Each drama has certain challenges to be met, and the candidate is rewarded by receiving particular strengths or positive character traits in return. Based upon the Alice A. Bailey book of the same name; other sources sometimes change the order of the Labours.

right action. A blessing to benefit the soul and body assisting the indwelling consciousness to proceed toward right action, which may manifest in renewed health or easy transition. Last Rites include communion at times, the use of holy oils, holy water, candles, and prayers to assist in the creation of a sacred atmosphere. *See* Healing rites.

Laya Yoga. *See* Yoga.

Laying on of hands. Techniques of spiritual healing wherein direct contact is used.

Leadbeater, Charles Webster. b. Cheshire, England, 1854, d. 1934. Author, clairvoyant, student of theosophy, and colleague of Annie Besant in the early work of the Theosophical Society. In 1893, under spiritual guidance, he began what was to become a life-long investigation into the phenomenon of clairvoyance. *The Masters and the Path,* his most important work, described what Dr. Besant called the "Perfected Men, the Masters, the Men beyond Mankind," and the steps to be taken on the spiritual path to reach that eminence, from probation to acceptance as disciples, and beyond. In later work with Besant, the phenomenon of auras was explored, and the authors reproduced in color many different forms they had seen, some evoked by listening to music, some apparent in people experiencing a specific human emotion, some even seen emanating from buildings where crowds had gathered. Both Leadbeater and Besant maintained that Gautama, the Buddha, had previously incarnated as other great spiritual teachers: Hermes, Zoroaster, and Orpheus. Leadbeater is considered to have been a pioneer in the evolution of new thought exploration. *The Masters and the Path*, 1946; *Thought-Forms;* 1911; *The Chakras: A Monograph,* 1972.

Leadership. Agni virtue for Cancer. The hand that rocks the cradle rules the world, we are told. Similarly, "We build a lighted house and dwell therein." Someday we will realize that the power we gained in purifying our own life is needed for the planet. We are ready, for now we know the world is our home and leadership is the work.

Left-hand path. Building personality and its attachments (versus right-hand mystical ascent) which leads to stronger ego and more experience on the outer–physical and material–to free us of karma or to dissolve the barriers within the nonself. *See* Right-hand path; Evolution.

Left hemisphere (of brain). One part of the NEOCORTEX (the third brain). Its unique characteristics are rational thought, the ability to analyze, judge, and evaluate. Relates comfortably to the outer world and its secular standards. The goal of the disciple is to be able to utilize both left and right hemispheres and to be able to discern which is appropriate for a needed application. This particular talent is called DISCERNMENT.

Lemuria. A fabled land said to predate Atlantis, located in the Pacific Ocean region, that met with destruction. Some inhabitants are said to have survived by fleeing to other areas. Lemurians are considered a ROOT RACE or GROUP MIND that emerged from the etheric and formed the first physical bodies of humanity especially sensitive to the astral/feeling nature. This ancient area often is referred to as the Land of Mu.

Lent. This season begins on Ash Wednesday and lasts for forty days, not counting Sundays. Jesus spent forty days in the wilderness, thinking and praying. Christians spend extra time reviewing their lives, their lessons, and planning how they may return God's love by helping others. The color for Lent is purple, as we show repentance for our mistakes and sorrow for the way Jesus was treated. Holy Week starts with Palm Sunday. We recall the story of Jesus' ride into Jerusalem on a donkey, the people cheering. Maundy Thursday reminds of his Last Supper with his friends. The chalice and the wafer are symbols of the wine and bread. The color for Good Friday is black to show grief and sadness for Jesus' death on the cross.

"Let the dead bury the dead." (Matthew 8.22) Let the unawakened–not physically dead but not alive to higher consciousness–take care of the dead; or, those of the same level of consciousness are to care for one another. Let those who are aware care for those likewise awakened to the greater life. Awareness separates people into either "dead" or "alive."

Leys. Currents of energy flowing within the Earth, invisible to scientific instruments but discernible through attunement. Just as the human body has energy channels (meridians), so the body of Mother Earth has energy lines. Just as every living being is animated by the life force, so too is the Earth. Ancient stone monuments are sometimes felt to be grand acupuncture needles–gathering, purifying, and increasing these teeming energies. Dowsing and other sensitivity techniques are used to detect, measure, and evaluate leys. (The more common term, "ley lines," is redundant.)

Life review. An evaluation of one's life–whether done while physically alive or from the spirit perspective after physical death.

Light. A degree of electrical energy which, when condensed, forms matter.

Light being. A spirit of high vibration or holy presence, without form and often without specific identity. Related to near-death experiences and contact with the light and apparitions.

Light body. The body created through the transformation of the astral body and of desire into aspiration, leading the disciple into transfiguration. Transfiguration is possible through the electric fire of the SPIRITUAL TRIAD which pours into the personality levels through the processes of advanced meditation and contemplation. The light of the Spiritual Triad works through the higher mind, stimulating the release of the lights of the atoms of the three bodies of the personality and producing enlightenment or transfiguration. In this achievement the astral body is cleared of all its glamours, and the illusions of the mental body are washed away, allowing the individual to stand in the light of the Spiritual Triad. The human soul makes itself ready to wear this "robe of glory." As the light body is woven or built, the astral body disintegrates and we are able to enter into more direct communication with the intuitional plane, home of the soul. Light, as illumination, produces the ability to mediate, referred to as Ray 3; the color generally attributed to Ray 3 is yellow.

Light workers. Those who perceive the light of higher consciousness and seek to both amplify and express that higher consciousness through themselves and in harmony with that awareness.

Lily. This symbol of virginity, purity, and chastity when portrayed with saints or sages also represents the Virgin Mary and the annunciation of Jesus, or at Easter the purity of Christ and the resurrection–life renewed.

Lipikas. Lofty DEVAS who serve as deities to guide human beings in how to work with the forces of nature. LORDS OF KARMA, a common reference, is not quite appropriate for these are more the points of consciousness in the mighty forces that move as currents through embodied life, allowing individuals to respond to the flow. Each person records within his or her own higher nature the use of these energies and will balance the karmic account in the process of evolving toward higher awareness.

Living Ethics. This Agni term im- plies living according to the high standard of spirituality we set for ourselves, i.e., to fulfill the themes and disciplines to which we are committed. The Agni yogi is to live out the teachings in the midst of daily duty and responsibility. Agni Yoga is often called "Ethical Living."

"Living in the now." An expression to encourage staying centered in the current events of life–one day at a time, one moment at a time–rather than dwelling on the past or exaggerating expectations of the future. Being with the opportunity each moment presents; also known as "being fully present."

Lodge. The organized Hierarchy of humanity, also called White Lodge or BROTHERHOOD.

Logoi, the seven planetary. The seven great CHOHANS serving the Christ and the planetary Plan, guiding and guarding planetary life and all points of consciousness evolving within this domain. All religions reference these guiding Wise Ones who serve the SOLAR LOGOS in some specific terms, i.e., Christianity, the "ELDER BROTHERS BEFORE THE THRONE"; Buddhism, the "seven Great Rishis," etc.

Logos. The Greek title given to the Great Creator of All; literally the "Word," reminding us that the Word went forth and set all into motion.

Lords: Fire, Flame (or Love), Form, Individuality, Karma, Mercury, Mind, Wisdom. *See* Celestial hierarchies.

Lords of Compassion. The name given to those tender influences of the higher world that work to assist in time of trials, particularly working with feminine energies, and seeming to work under the DIVINE FEMININE influence. The term comes from its correlation with the BODHISATTVA OF COMPASSION, KUAN YIN, and the Eastern tradition.

Lords of the Law. The three guides of the created worlds: the MANU, the BODHISATTVA, and the MAHACHOHAN. These beings hold the blueprint for the Plan's unfolding. They constitute the spiritual triad of the planet.

Lots Of Vital Energy. These words form the acronym LOVE, implying love is much more expansive, much more powerful, much more vital than readily acknowledged.

Lotus. A flower of the East of great beauty. It grows out of swampy areas with its roots in muck and holds itself above the water and open to the light. Used as a symbol of the soul that opens to the light in full array of beauty after the personality – with its roots in Earth matter is nourished by the emotional waters of the astral nature and guided by the structure of the mind – breaks through into clarity. It represents both beauty and achievement.

Lotus posture. A specific HATHA YOGA posture used for centuries as a resting or centering point.

Lotus with three pearls. This logo has been adapted by the author's  Sancta Sophia Seminary to symbolize a wholeness of consciousness that can emerge from three pearls of wisdom: Kabalah, Esoteric Christianity, and Agni Yoga.

Love. Four levels of love–EROS, PHILIA, HUMANITARIAN *(humanus),* and AGAPÉ – correlate closely to the chakras. Since the evolution of love is its principal work, Christianity is often considered a school of BHAKTI YOGA; while closely related, it is not. Bhakti is a Ray 6 approach, Christianity a Ray 2 approach born in a Ray 6 age. We could say Christianity has a Ray 6 personality and a Ray 2 soul.

Love is the Agni virtue for Leo. Not just attraction or emotion but the energy that sustains all life–Lots Of Vital Energy. As the heart opens, we become generous and sharing, a conduit for the higher forces of life and empowered to step down this life-giving flow for the benefit of all. It is the nature of the disciple to love and to care.

Love-wisdom. Exemplifies "thinketh in the heart," a goal for the spiritual aspirant who is integrating the three vehicles of personality. An appropriate reminder is presented as "behind emotion lives feeling and behind intellect is knowing." The two points of duality (feeling and knowing) must integrate until we love with the mind and know with the heart. Then love-wisdom, Ray 2, results in maintaining that which has been created. Its color is blue.

Low self-esteem. A barrier to soul expression created by distorted thoughts and feelings regarding the nature of our being. This confused field of awareness blocks the light of the soul from penetrating to awareness, thereby misrepresenting the impressions and perceptions of our worth and the value of our contribution. A distinct barrier to illumination.

Lower bodies. The three vehicles of expression vibrating in the denser world of personality, i.e., physical form, emotional nature, and lower mental body.

Lower mind. The three lower levels of the mental body where old instinctual thinking of the species, as well as personal programming, exists – as do the imprints of early unconscious life and the home of the rational processing mind. These lower vibrating frequencies establish the foundation for "thinking" in personality. Also known as the nonself, indicating an identity with personality rather than Creator.

Lower self. *See* Basic self.

Lucid dreaming. A simultaneous, dual state of consciousness – dream-state and awake-state. Awareness of dreaming while asleep and within the dream, often with the ability to control the dream action.

Lucifer. Called an angel in the Bible, a LIGHT BEING who led souls seeking to experience in the denser world in the DESCENT INTO MATTER. The name means "light."

Lu Luz. Mayan for "light," as in enlightenment. A term used for the light of high consciousness and awareness that comes as the blessings of a golden age. Maya wisdomkeepers often speak with reverence about the Aquarian Age as the "time of Lu Luz."

Lunar body. A lower form where the history of human EVOLUTION is stored in the PERMANENT ATOMS. The Moon is the celestial form called the lunar body; however, the human ASTRAL BODY is also referred to as the lunar body.

Lunar initiation. A period during the involutionary process in which the development of humanity's astral senses was emphasized. Progress was achieved by an evolving humanity discovering awareness of the Plan through the unfolding of astral senses so that humanity could develop feeling and learn to guide personal emotion rather than be ruled by the instinctual nature. Those who achieved INITIATION became the forerunners for mass consciousness.

Lunar mysteries. The mysteries–or unseen powers, patterns, and influences–that ruled the planet throughout the involutionary period. Through these great laws and forces, humanity and all the kingdoms were consciously guided, influenced, and stimulated in such a way that all life was pulled into the denser desire nature. The unconscious, passionate, instinctual nature empowered in this lunar phase still vigorously affects all life, primarily on a subconscious level.

Lunatic. From the Latin word *luna* meaning "Moon"–indicative of the belief that fluctuations of sanity related to phases of the Moon. One so affected by lunar forces that the rational mind suffers from a loss of control and from imbalance.

M

Macrocosm. The great universe, or cosmos; the big picture or magnificent view of life from a cosmic perspective. A system that reflects one of its components on a large scale, e.g., the cosmos reflects the life of humanity; humanity reflects the life of a single person; a single person represents the life of a single cell–only functioning on a larger scale. Macrocosm/microcosm reflects the law of "As ABOVE, SO BELOW."

Magic. The art and practice of changing consciousness at will. The conscious direction of mind and will to accomplish a spiritual goal.

Magnetic healers. A category of world servers integrating the forces of head, heart, and ajna (brow center).

Magnetized consciousness. When we are charged with aspiration and a passionate desire to know, we, by an act of will, can focus on a word or phrase that becomes the nucleus of all attention. This word or phrase being so charged begins to draw thoughts and ideas of the same essence, or vibration, to itself like a magnet.

Mahabharata. The great epic of Hindu scriptures of which the *Bhagavad Gita* is only a part.

Mahachohan. Also called the Great Chohan, the Lord of Civilization, the head of all adepts, and the Lord of Ray 3 of active intelligence, or the intelligence aspect of deity. As head of the third great department of the planetary hierarchy, he presides over the activities of the four minor Rays, their Masters, and the synthesizing Ray. This Great Being, responsible for manifestation of the principle of intelligence for an entire world period, assumes the duty of developing a great civilization. The embodiment for the planet of the third, or intelligence, aspect of deity.

Maharishi Mahesh Yogi. b. India, 1918, d. n.d. Indian physicist and founder of TRANSCENDENTAL MEDITATION (TM), a discipline for turning the attention inward, allowing us to "effortlessly transcend thinking and gain the status of pure awareness." He compares the human mind to an ocean with constant wave activity on its surface, expressed as thoughts, emotions, perceptions–but profoundly still at its depths. Guru Dev, Maharishi's teacher in the Himalayas for twelve years, taught him the ancient meditation technique of the Vedas, which is used to explore these depths of human consciousness, now known as Transcendental Meditation. The Science of Creative Intelligence was derived from TM in part as a discipline for discovering therapies to treat the damaging effects of stress in the present day. *The Science of Being and the Art of Living,* 1966; *A Message: Creative Intelligence,* 1970.

Mahasamadhi. The great rest or sleep, meaning the great peace, death, or higher reality. *Maha,* "large" or "great"; *samadhi,* "peace."

Mahat. Holy Spirit (feminine); that spiritual power residing in matter which responds to the charge of fohat (masculine), resulting in creative activity.

Maitreya. A visible proxy on Earth of the invisible deity; often used as a symbol of mind or thought, especially in regard to divine mind. The Christ. In Eastern spiritual traditions the guiding consciousness that permeates humanity with an awakening of the God-within. Specifically, the anticipated incarnation of the Buddha to restore Buddhist dharma–expected to occur some 2500 years after Buddha's passing. The time given for the reappearance is at the beginning of the AQUARIAN AGE. This WORLD TEACHER, Head of HIERARCHY–similar to the ESOTERIC Christian use of the Christ, Teacher of Angels and Humanity–is known also as the BODHISATTVA, Imam Mahdi, and the Prince of Peace.

Mala beads. A set of uniform beads upon which prayers are counted to invoke spiritual power; used in the Eastern tradition.

Malkuth. The tenth sephirah on the kabalistic TREE OF LIFE equates to the dense world of form (the lowest vibration on the Tree) and is called the "kingdom."

Mammalian brain. The level of brain that relates one thing to another; the mammal portion that develops social responses and bonding. *See* Neocortex; Reptilian brain; Three-brain concept.

Man. The English word is derived from *manas* (Sanskrit) meaning "to think." Humanity is thus called the race of man, denoting the thinking, evolving kingdom–not a reference to maleness. Each human is to balance masculine and feminine energies and, under the guidance of mind (manas), know how to use these forces for the good of all kingdoms evolving on planet Earth.

Manas. A Sanskrit word meaning "to think," refers to the mind-principle of the human. That which distinguishes the human from the lower kingdoms: reasoning faculty, intelligence, understanding, individual mind, powers of attention, and choice. Humanity is to evolve the mind for the planet. *Kama manas* refers to lower mind, the Sanskrit *kama* meaning "desire."

Mandala. A diagram either imagined or actually depicted; typically a circle or square containing a cen-

tral symbol. A design or symmetrical pattern used for meditation  and contemplation and intended to balance and attune our energies to a higher influence. It represents the enclosure of sacred space and penetration to the divine center and assists the integration of cosmic intelligence. Both a pattern of existence and a system on which meditative visualization is based.

Manifestation. A form in which someone or something, e.g., an individual, a divine being, or an idea, is revealed. Also, the action of bringing the realities of more subtle planes into matter or form.

Manser, Ann. b. United States, date unknown, d. 1976. Spiritualist teacher, artist, and co-author with Cecil North of the *Pages of Shustah Card Book.* Most widely known for her "aurascopes," written, detailed auric analyses of individual force fields surrounding both human beings and animals. With no information other than the name, sex, and, if animal, the species, Ms. Manser was able to determine "the health, problems, karmic involvements, degree of spiritual development, evolutional status, past conditioning, and future indications insofar as they are impressed upon the auric field of the personality under investigation." Her entire life was dedicated to investigations of the areas of auras, color, force fields, evolutions of the kingdoms, and the Holy Kabalah. Ms. Manser was an active supporter of the Temple of the Living God in St. Petersburg, Florida, an interfaith, nonsectarian religious and educational church-center, researching metaphysics and philosophy, with emphasis upon uniting religion and science.

Mantra. A word or phrase arranged rhythmically to generate certain vibrations when sounded. The sound itself is understood to express and be one with the divinity invoked by words of power. The mantra spoken to the subconscious repeatedly, aloud or silently–in prayer, incantation, or meditation–focuses heart and mind upon a certain guiding principle to reprogram to new awareness. Mantras associated with a specific energy, teacher, or group are intoned to receive spiritual guidance and strength.

Mantra Yoga. *See* Yoga.

Manu. Also known as the Lord of the World. The title of the office in the planetary hierarchy filled by a Great One who serves as the ruler and founder of a great plan and builder of a human root race, continents, flora, civilizations, and nations. Guides the work of the BODHISATTVA and the MAHACHOHAN for a particular period, working with forms through which Spirit is to manifest–destroying and rebuilding: evolving. The Manu represents and embodies one of three aspects of divine manifestation, the Ray 1 aspect of creative will. The three great guides of the human race are the Mahachohan, the Bodhisattva, and the Manu.

Marian Year. The year dedicated to Mary for her intercession on behalf of humanity; 1987 was declared by Pope John Paul as the Marian Year for Peace.

MariEl. A spiritual healing system developed by Ethel Lombardi of Locksport, Illinois, in the 1980s. She received the procedure from spirit and taught the approach to many throughout the United States.

Marriage. As a Christian sacrament, this holy ceremony is conducted by a minister or priest, as God's representative. Two, who have prepared spiritually, take vows of love and dedication to each other before the community of spiritual believers of which they are a part. A relationship both legal and spiritual wherein each party pledges a commitment to both the physical and nonphysical levels of union. Each pledges to support and participate in an agreed-upon lifestyle. Marriage is a discipline referred to in the Bible, wherein it is stated, "Be ye not unequally yoked together with unbelievers." (2 Corinthians 6.14 KJV) Esoterically, this means the initiated should not be wed to the uninitiated because the values and goals are disparate.

Mary, the Blessed Virgin. The mother of Jesus and great feminine disciple who served the Christ ministry as esoteric head of the tradition until her translation and assumption into heavenly spheres at the close of her Earth life. Proclaimed "Queen of Heaven and Earth," she continues to serve as a mother to all humanity and as a Master of Ray 7. Presently she is very active in both the inner and the outer worlds, providing guidance and protection for those who align themselves to the Divine. "Mother Mary" is a Christian term of endearment for the mother of Jesus after she was given to all humanity as mother of all by the Christ on the Cross, when he commanded, "Behold, thy Mother."

Mother Mary embodies and represents the divine feminine archetype.

Masculine principle. The masculine aspect of God, usually called the Father, especially concerned with will, intellect, or law. Humanity has developed this aspect of its nature to an extent of abuse, so that in the present day the major energies have shifted to feminine to return planetary life to a point of balance. The great principle of gender requires all life to express both masculine and feminine qualities.

Maslow, Abraham. b. New York City, 1908, d. 1970. Humanist psychologist who postulated that the higher needs that appear to arise in the human being after basic survival needs are met are the result of an inner pressure towards a fuller expression of being–a self-actualization–in the same naturalistic sense that an acorn may be said to be pressing toward becoming an oak tree. Maslow and his contemporaries saw the technique of transcendental meditation as a means of achieving extraordinary human growth, creativity, and fulfillment. *Toward a Psychology of Being,* 1968; *Religions, Values, and Peak Experiences,* 1970.

Mass thinking. Group mind that produces form and programming.

Master

One who, having mastered the lower levels of self, has developed an individual consciousness or recognition of oneness with God. Called "Master" of high consciousness because he or she accepts students to guide their personal development by sharing energy and wisdom. In the Western esoteric tradition, a fifth degree initiate–one who has achieved self-mastery, thus making personality a vehicle to express the higher nature. Eastern tradition refers to the third initiation as "Master." Many Masters stand ready to give guidance to all of humanity who seek it.

Master Djwhal Khul, "The Tibetan." A teaching Master of RAY 2 who has provided humanity with nearly 10,000 pages of teachings through his AMANUENSIS, ALICE A. BAILEY, with whom he was in subjective communication from 1919 until she passed on in 1949. His telepathic dictations conveying esoteric thought were subsequently published in twenty volumes by Lucis Trust.

Master Hilarion. Master of Ray 5, science and exactness. He is said to have established spiritualism as a way humanity may perceive and study on-going life in the nonphysical realms. Believed to have been St. Paul in a previous incarnation; today at work in Egypt.

Communicant: David Anrias, *Through the Eyes of the Masters,* 1932.

Master Jesus. The Great Initiate who serves as wayshower for the Christian tradition for his service to the Christ and his example to all humanity; a Master on the 6th Ray of devotion. Joshua, son of Nun, in a previous incarnation, and Jesus of Nazareth who surrendered his body to be used by the Christ. Thought to be living today in Syria.

Master Kuthumi (or Koot Humi). A Master on Ray 2, love-wisdom, the blending of heart and mind, the Ray on which the Lord Christ vibrates. Love-wisdom is to integrate heart and mind and originates as will-to-unite. PYTHAGORAS in one of his previous incarnations. Residing today at Shigatse, the monastery of the Tashi Lama in Tibet.

Master Morya. The Chohan of Ray 1, creative will, also known as El Morya. He is said to be the influence encouraging the establishment of esoteric schools throughout the world in this period of transition. A Rajput prince believed to have occupied the Mogul Emperor Akbar's body in a previous incarnation. He now resides at Shigatse.

Master Saint Germain. Master of the 7th Ray of orderliness. Said to have appeared first in 1561 and to have subsequently undertaken several incarnations, particularly among theosophists. *See* Germain, Comte de Saint.

Master Serapis. The Master of Ray 3, active intelligence, is now working with the devic evolution. In telepathic communication with author David Anrias, Serapis has said that in the imminent merging of Uranus and Aquarius, "humanity has pos-sibilities of spiritual development so vast and comprehensive as to precipitate a great change in the future of the whole race, when a new religion will be evolved uniting the spiritual and the scientific elements."

Master, The Venetian. Master of Ray 4, harmony through conflict, and the painter Paul Veronese in one of his previous incarnations. He has communicated that in the coming new Age of Enlightenment, "art, once handmaiden of religion, but in this materialistic age completely divorced from it, will again fulfill its highest function, that of inspiring reverence in the beholder." The Venetian Master will be cooperator with Serapis in training the artistic mind of the future.

Masters of Wisdom. Members of the adept brotherhood; those who have evolved through the human experience and now act as guides for humanity. Similar to ELDER BROTHERS.

Materia Lucida. An Agni term. The waves of luminous matter containing the consciousness of the cosmic Rays that gradually dawn into new light as enlightenment occurs. Materia Lucida is called a "curling chaos," a "knowing spirit," and appears as "the harp of light," denoting differently to varying states of consciousness. Also, known as the "Mother of the World" and "Cosmic Love." We are introduced to the idea of space as not empty but as a womb of subtle ethers having received the sparks of FOHAT and nurturing them to high consciousness. Materia Lucida is revealed as the matter aspect of the original energy-matter. So all matter originates in primal form, the true nature of which is light, consciousness, and love. HELENA ROERICH in Vol. 1 of her *Letters* says, "Creative Materia Lucida serves as an embodiment for the high spirit." She reminds us that Materia Lucida is the outer garment or covering for the spirit on all levels of manifestation; form is then a covering over a "seed of psyche-life."

Materia matrix. An Agni term. The primary matter that does not penetrate to the earthly sphere because of the whirling of infected lower layers. But fohat, as granulation of primary matter, can reach the earthly surface in the form of sparks by the outflow of radiant matter, Materia Lucida. The realized sparks of fohat and the streams of Materia Lucida are benevolent, for they imbue the spirit with the urge of evolution.

Matter. The densified spirit that coagulates into building blocks containing receptive energy; or, intelligence awaiting ignition.

Maya. That which does not exist and is therefore illusory. The glamours, illusions, or delusions perceived by limited mind. The phenomenal universe; unreality; all that is finite, subject to decay and change; all that is not eternal and unchangeable; the world of appearance. The agreed-upon collective hypnosis of a culture, religion, or society that seeks to regulate the guidelines of behavior for its people. In the Hindu tradition, the Great Cosmic force responsible for the phenomena of material existence.

Maya (the culture). An ancient Mesoamerican high civilization of which little is known. The modern Maya people have little understanding of their illustrious past; however, it is believed the Maya culture followed the Olmec (200 B.C. until A.D. 900) with great influence. They calculate their history in a much longer cycle. Specialists in mathematics, time-keeping, and astronomy, they left an array of hieroglyphs, calendars temples, pyramids, and cities to be studied. The term *Maya* means "mother."

Meditation. A process which results in contact with high consciousness and the transfer of the human consciousness into that of soul awareness. A science that aids us in attaining a direct experience of God–usually through periods of silence in which the work of concentration, contemplation, and gestation brings about soul growth. Techniques vary; however, the goal is to be centered and receptive to spiritual knowledge and insight through contact with the God-within or high levels of consciousness. The technique of attuning our physical, emotional, and mental bodies to the spiritual source.

Medium. An individual who allows his or her personality vehicle to be receptive to temporary inhabitation by an intelligence without form.

Mediumistic tendencies. A particular sensitivity to astral energies or influences. People often discover they are easily influenced or take on the feelings or thoughts of others–usually believed to be a result of lunar mystery training or the lack of development of appropriate boundaries.

Mental body. Layers of mind built of frequencies, each of which contains a record in thought established as the soul evolved. The mental vehicle reworks, synthesizes, and integrates with the BUDDHI as awareness expands.

Mental plane. A band or frequency of vibration that organizes into ranges of knowing from instinctual and subconscious to intellectual and then subtle, abstract, intuitional knowing. The physical, mechanical organs of mind (three in number) are developed in humanity to translate the subtle frequencies of mind into outer functions.

Mental sub-planes. The seven sub-planes of the mental plane which is one of seven greater planes representing successive levels of consciousness, rates of vibration, or states of being within our universe. On the involutionary path of descent into matter, the self must descend the seven planes (each of which has seven sub-planes) and then progress back through these planes in order to return to the Infinite Source to realize divine oneness and immortality. From the "highest" to the "lowest" of what is called the cosmic physical plane of the universe, our universe is made up of these seven planes: logoic (or divine), monadic, atmic, buddhic (or intuitional), mental (or manasic), astral, and physical. All of the planes serve as bridges between the individual and the universe.

Mentalism (Hermetic principle of). "The ALL is MIND; the Universe is Mental" of *The Kybalion* embodies the belief that all matter is the mental creation of "THE ALL," in which mind we "live and move and have our being."

Mentor. A guide, teacher, GURU, or confessor. Someone who knows and takes another into apprenticeship.

Meridians (of physical body). Streams of energy that flow through physical body to keep CHI, or life force, distributed to all systems, organs, and cells that the vehicle of matter can relate to inhabiting spirit. If imbalanced or out of harmony, the flow is affected.

Mesmerism. The recall of techniques useful for exploring non-rational levels of mind. Rediscovery began with the work of Franz Mesmer (1734-1815), an Austrian physician, and the technique laid the foundation for hypnosis. Esoteric teachings suggest many earlier civilizations used altered states of consciousness and mesmerism/hypnosis in their cultures. The Atlanteans are said to have developed it to a high degree.

Messenger. An individual who delivers the word, or message; the word often refers to a prophet.

Messiah. In the Hebrew tradition, the long-awaited holy one–the God-Man–anointed and sent to the people by God the Almighty.

Metaphysics. The study of laws higher than the physical and dealing with universal truths to teach humanity to align with the purpose and plan of life.

Metempsychosis. An ancient Egyptian doctrine indicating the immediate passage of the soul at death into another body. An older word often incorrectly used as a synonym for REINCARNATION, but with a slightly different implication. *See* Pythagorus.

Microcosm. The little universe manifesting in and through the physical body of the human. Minute bits of consciousness that live, work, and express within this miniature universe. Acknowledgement of the smallest, seemingly microscopic particles in the processes of life, and of the roles they play.

Middle-road path. Having experienced both great riches and extreme austerity, the Buddha pronounced the middle-road path the safest route for most people as they advance to higher states of consciousness.

Millennium. A period of one thousand years. Currently we are entering the third millennium of Christianity, which is the cusp of the millennium.

Mind. The knowing of an individual or group that ranges from the lowest point of survival instinct to the most subtle waves of consciousness held in mind-stuff. In the human realm, mind extends from instinct to intellect to intuition and expresses itself through various ways of knowing. Brain is mechanism, not mind. *See* Group mind; Mental plane; Three worlds of mind.

"Mind is the slayer of the Real." An expression that denotes the ability of the rational mind to block, distort by rigidity, and hold us in bondage–not permitting reality to be expanded or truth perceived–through rejection of the more subtle realities of soul with its interlocking impressions, intuition, and gentle touches. When separation rules, rational mind resists inner truth.

Mind of Christ. Divine intelligent love, like the COSMIC CHRIST (the indwelling intelligence). When enlightened we develop mind: the clarity, balance, focus that Jesus, the historical Christ, displayed 2,000 years ago. "Let the mind that is in Christ Jesus be also in you." In modern language we might say, "what the Soul knows"–that we are one body/mind/soul and one with all others, all else. Another term is CLOUD OF KNOWABLE THINGS.

Mind of God. The Omni, all-knowing aspect of the Creator.

Mind screen. The projected point used to visualize pictures within the mind and developed by practice. Once the capability is achieved, the image-making mechanism of personality projects upon it. It is available to higher consciousness, i.e., High Self, Soul, or other intelligences.

Mind-stuff. The unformed mist, or fog, in the mental plane to be drawn together by the minds that can enter the subtler frequencies and exert a pull toward form reality. These become the mind builders or leaders for the expansion of consciousness for all of humanity.

Mir. The Russian word for "peace." A power word when spoken as a mantra.

Mithraism. The worship of Mithras, Persian god of light and guardian against evil, which flourished in the late Roman Empire, rivaling Christianity. Its central theme is that of Mithras killing the primordial bull, the first act of creation. In the West, the cult became a mystery religion with strong emphasis on blood atonement, fellowship, strict moral discipline, and a distinctive emphasis on dualism. Mithraism taught that the soul ascended through several realms and that there was personal salvation after death for the faithful and punishment for the wicked.

Monad. An indivisible and divine spiritual life-atom; the unified triad–atma, buddhi, manas. The immortal self within each person that lives on in successive incarnations, progressing to the stature of the adept beyond which extends unlimited evolution. The spark of divine life, that highest part of the constitution of beings. The innermost self, the source of life and light that nurtures the unfolding soul. This true self, a breath of the Absolute, is in no way influenced by conditional, finite existence of the personality. The immortal and eternal principle within us–an **indivisible** part of the integral whole–the Universal Spirit from which it emanates and into which it will be absorbed. Any self-contained system of any size which, if divided, ceases to exist as such; whereas, if absorbed into a larger system, it becomes a part of a greater monad.

Money. Concretized energy, its value to be used with discrimination.

Moon sign. The astrological position calculated with specific formulas revealing the constellation in which the Moon was located at the time of one's birth. One of the three most important personal placements in an individual's chart, i.e., Sun, Moon and ascendant.

Morphogenetic field. A term coined by Rupert Sheldrake of Great Britain as he studied the life field that exists around each individual life form. The concept is focused on etheric reality; major examinations or studies are now being conducted by physicists as they venture into realms formerly known as MYSTICISM.

Mother Earth. A title for the Earth, showing respect and love for the service she has rendered. Called "mother" for her life-giving properties, Earth is considered feminine in the mystery tradition because she is receptive to other intelligences evolving through her created form. Among Native Americans the Creative Principle and source of supply for life's preservation. All needs are met from the bosom of Mother Earth; therefore planet Earth must be treated with respect and honored as the life-giver by all who dwell thereon. The World Mother, known in many traditions, is "a virgin pure as the snow on the mountains, as beautiful as the most colorful lilies, and as wise as Mother Earth." It is her mission to establish the brotherhood of men and the sisterhood of women all over the world.

Mother of the World. A reference to the divine feminine–particularly prevalent in Agni Yoga writings but used by many systems of thought.

Mother principle. The feminine principle in creation; the Mother aspect of the Deity; that receptive part that accepts the spirit aspect in order to manifest in matter. A cosmic force that leavens and nurtures.

"Mother, the." *See* Richards, Mira.

"Movement and measure, All is." A Maya reference to their great

deity, Hunab K'U, who is called the creator of movement and measure.

Mudras. A Sanskrit word referring to certain positions of the fingers and hands used in devotional yoga or in exoteric religious worship to convey emotions and blessings. These positions are considered by oriental mystics to have particular esoteric significance and are found both in Buddhist and Hindu religious art throughout India and Northern Asia. Mudras are used in a psychophysical process in yoga in order to seal the energy and attention of the practitioner.

Music of the Spheres. The tones of the creative currents flowing from the cosmic song, or silent sound. Commonly thought of as emanating from heaven or the higher astral becoming audible as the tones densify. Heavenly voices or songs heard in mystical moments.

Myth. A parable or legend told to preserve an understanding of truth. Since it is often esoteric or difficult to grasp, it is best shared or disguised by being cloaked within a story; thus the message is protected and preserved until its hearers can detect its meaning. Teaching myths have guided the minds of humanity throughout all cultures for thousands of years. The term does not mean untruthful, although it is sometimes translated that way.

Mysteries. Truths that cannot be realized when we simply are told. While they are not secrets, they must be pondered in order for the Great Truth to be revealed. Truths are unveiled from within or not at all; the outer consciousness prepares itself through meditation and contemplation for the revelation of the mysteries of life.

Mysteries of Isis. Secret teachings of Ancient Egypt regarding the Mother of Osiris. The deity referred to as Mother of Humanity (pre-Christian).

Mystery school. A place where teachings and techniques prepare individuals for the process of inner development. No outer structure can assure inner success, but such an environment is constructed and assistance rendered in specific ways to facilitate progress in expansion of consciousness.

Mystery teachings. Hidden truths revealed to those who can penetrate to the inner temples or teachers and share these truths to help others understand the laws of life and how to live in harmony with these realized high principles.

Mystic. A person with an awareness of a multidimensional reality who usually seeks to have a personal relationship with God. The mystic is considered a blend of the ORPHIC and the OCCULTIST.

Mystic Christian. An individual who seeks to know oneness with the Christ through experience rather than through dogma and commandment. The consciousness becomes attuned to the essence of the way and is nurtured by inner contact with the Christ and the mystical body of oneness.

Mystic marriage. The state of consciousness that unites the heart and mind of an initiate, transforming the nature of both.

Mystic way. A path of devotion and service to the cause of God as made known to the individual through an inner connection to the divine.

Mystical body of Christ. The second Person of the Trinity, the logos, who gives form to life by descending into matter. Through the sacrifice inherent in assuming the limitations of matter, the logos has become the "heavenly being" in whom all forms exist and of whose body all forms are a part. Also, the mystical consciousness held at the intuitive, buddhic, or CHRIST CONSCIOUSNESS level that awakens the unfolding spirit within each person, and the realization of the unity to all of life in God by virtue of the Christ spirit.

Mysticism. The practice of direct union with the divine. The practice of experiences designed to facilitate direct contact with the eternal and invisible oneness. Mystics pursue the study of these experiences through love and devotion.

N

Nadis. Numerous points created by lines of energy crossing and criss-crossing in the etheric, or energy, nonphysical body. In esoteric thought, inherited from the wisdom of the East, each body is believed to have a number of nadis, or energy pressure points, to help the body maintain good circulation and balance.

Nails. Because of their use in the crucifixion, nails appearing in religious symbology represent Jesus' physical suffering.

Namasté. A Hindu greeting translated informally as "the Presence within me greets the Presence within you."

Narcissism. Excessive love of one-self.

Native. Natural to a given area; astrologically, a Sun sign area.

Near-death experience (NDE). A self-explanatory term used when an individual has moved to and beyond the brink but returns to outer consciousness, often aware of a new dimension of life. This so-called death experience awakens the awareness of life's continuity, and new values of a different nature register upon the experiencer to be integrated into the personality life upon return. A scientific study in the 1970s brought these profound happenings to public awareness as a result of Dr. Raymond Moody's *Life After Life*. It was estimated in 1993 that about 13.5 million people in the United States have had such an experience.

Neocortex. This latest stage of development in the physical brain consists of two hemispheres capable of communication and coworking. The right hemisphere relates to the whole of life, and the left analyzes and evaluates. This level of brain activity produces measurable intelligence quotient (I.Q.).

Neo-Paganism. A modern Earth religion that borrows and adapts from pre-Christian Pagan religions, sometimes with additions from contemporary religious thinkers.

Neo-Pentecostal. A modern term referring to current interest in the phenomena of the GIFTS OF THE SPIRIT, as expressed in psychic abilities and MYSTICISM.

Netzach. The seventh sephirah on the kabalistic Tree of Life, denoting victory, is considered the home of natural passions.

New Adam. Born of a divine idea through the overshadowing of the Holy Spirit. Often this title denotes the emerging, new, more-aware human on the path of EVOLUTION back to the Source, as is given in the New Testament. The Christ modeled a new human being with a consciousness humanity is now considered capable of attaining.

New Age. This term refers less to a time period than to a state of consciousness. The new awakening consciousness expressed through thoughts and actions reflecting an awareness of the Plan and realization of the divinity and oneness of humanity and all of life. A shift in consciousness characterized by a global perspective and attention to universal questions and problems. Unity, synthesis, intellectual development, scientific discovery, and ethical or spiritual living are keynotes of the present new era. Often specifically refers to the Age of Aquarius presently upon us, but indeed Master Jesus was "New Age" when he stood as a model of the new way made possible.

New Group of World Servers. Recently (1990) advised to drop the "new" since adequate numbers of world servers have identified themselves for a measurable period of time to anchor the will, dedication, and service necessary to bring forward the work of the HIERARCHY. The terminology was given to the world by the MASTER DJWHAL KHUL in the BAILEY materials (Lucis Trust).

New Jerusalem. A prototype city in the ethers that is the home of spiritual beings; also thought of as SHAMBALLA in Eastern teachings.

New Moon. A phase of the physical Moon when lunar influences assist in rapid new growth–a time for planting new thoughts, beginning anew, and being receptive to changes in one's life.

New paradigm. A fresh model, idea, or awareness; a revelation in formation; a possibility in process of being realized, e.g., the immanent potential of humanity coming into form.

Nightly review. In this exercise practiced before sleep, we review the day backward to capture situations needing repair or resolution. Considered an important discipline for serious students, this practice copes with mishandled situations daily rather than permitting an accumulation to be confronted after death.

Night of Brahma. *See* Pralaya.

Nirmanakaya. Advanced entities working with all evolving life, within karmic boundaries, from "spirit" rather than "form" side of life; related to wisdom, energies, and influences behind the manifested side of life.

Nirvana. Liberation; conscious absorption in the one divine life of the cosmos. The ultimate and absolute existence or state of consciousness attained by those who have achieved supreme perfection and holiness through the destruction of the limitations which prohibit recognition of the real Self. The annihilation of separative thoughts, intentions, and motives.

Those who have attained this stage of absorption in pure Cosmic Being have progressed through evolution so far along the Path that the personality has become thoroughly impersonalized without loss of consciousness. More specifically, personal and individual absorption, or identification with the true and divine Self–perfect peace. The state of freedom from karma, extinction of desire, passion, illusion, and the empirical self.

Noetic. Pertaining to or originating in the intellect; from the Greek word *noesis,* meaning understanding.

Nonrelease. This barrier to illumination is also known as attachment, with additional nuances; also, unforgivingness.

Nonself. The ego – the unreal, misguided, false self.

Nonsense. The mischief in which we engage when we allow the senses of the nonself to guide us in life experiences even though we may learn through them.

Nostradamus, Michel de. b. St. Remy, 1503, d. 1566. French astrologer, seer, and physician to Charles IX and Catherine de Medici. A collection of his apocalyptic prophecies in two volumes

129

> **Numerology.** The study and spiritual understanding of the vibration of numbers, rhythms, and cycles. A science of self-discovery that helps us comprehend the uniqueness of life, keys to personal karma, and how to identify talents and purposes. Rudimentary characteristics of numbers are:
>
> **1** will, initiating power, striving
> **2** love-wisdom, maintaining, humanity
> **3** active intelligence, mediating, creativity
> **4** conflict, foundation, future
> **5** exactness, change, freedom
> **6** devotion, family, harmony
> **7** spirituality, right-relationship, community
> **8** power, resources, responsibility
> **9** universality, joy, service
> **0** higher expression of the quality of the number it accompanies

of rhymed quatrains (1555-1558), though often enigmatic, appear to foretell events of the French Revolution, the two world wars, struggles in the Mideast, the Kennedy assassinations, the fall of communism in Russia, and the emergence of the Antichrist. In July of 1999, the "King of Terror" is prophesied to appear, heralding the end of the world as we know it. *The True Centuries,* 1558.

No-Thing. The unmanifest.

Novena. Meaning "ninefold." A nine-day prayer series usually for a specific intention. Both Christian and Eastern religions encourage novenas.

Numen. A spirit inhabiting natural phenomena, places, or objects. Also, creative genius.

Numinous. Charged with an indwelling light incapable of being described or comprehended and not necessarily noticeable from without. Pertaining to the supernatural or spiritually elevated nature.

Obedience. A vow taken by a subordinate in spiritual life in return for initiation or admittance to a desired tradition. A pledge of obedience is spiritually binding upon the CHELA and the initiator until both agree to dissolve the oath or when spiritual development of the "younger" has developed to such a degree that both realize through guidance or high consciousness the time for release has come. Many continue to love and obey long after the formal need for allegiance has passed. The initiator carries the spiritual responsibility for the chela's development and answers to the inner world while the vow is intact. The wiser is charged by the law of karma for errors; the chela is only responsible for obedience or disobedience.

Observer. A name given to the witness consciousness created through objectivity and spiritual insight; also sometimes called the KNOWER.

Obstacles on the path, four. The four greatest impediments to seekers of high consciousness are enumerated as MAYA, GLAMOURS, ILLUSIONS, and the DWELLER ON THE THRESHOLD. *See individual entries.*

Occult. That which is hidden, or occluded, and must be studied to be understood. In Latin, "to conceal," formed with the prefix *oc* meaning "reversely, inversely, opposite, and against." The opposite of "cult" because its philosophy teaches each to do his/her own thinking. The word may be used to correlate to the study of universal phenomena, but the true study of occultism seeks to penetrate the causal mysteries of being.

Occult memory. That which is held in subconscious–out of sight and out of mind–of either an individual or group, i.e., humanity.

Occult path. A way of inner embracing; intense purification of the nature.

Occult truths. Realities that lie behind the apparent and are comprehended only gradually as we continue to see the "cause" side of life.

Occultism. The science of life or universal nature; inner orientation to God; the need to know. Occult studies are those hidden or not known to most of humanity. An occult science not only includes the physical, psychic, mental, and spiritual part of the human being but also studies the structure, operation, origin, and destiny of the cosmos–also called the HERMETIC PRINCIPLES or ESOTERIC sciences. The occult was known as the KABALAH in the West and MYSTICISM, MAGIC, and YOGA philosophy in the East. Studies also include ESOTERIC PSYCHOLOGY and magic (both black and white); making contact with MASTERS, spacials, and devas; and trance work, including mediumship. Those on the path are expected to realize dedication, purification, discipline, teaching, and service. These teachings were hidden from the selfish-educated and uneducated as a precaution so the divine sciences would not be misused or turned into black magic. Occult traditions include the mystery schools of Egypt, Greece, and Rome, and initiatory traditions of secret societies such as the ROSICRUCIANS and FREEMASONRY.

Occultist. A person who studies the mystery (concealed, mystic) side of life, seeking to "know" the hidden wisdom.

Officials of the Seven Rays. The CHOHANS and MASTERS who exemplify the qualities of the RAYS and guide the seven streams of divine energy flowing from the Godhead.

Olive branch. This universally accepted symbol of peace represents God's recon-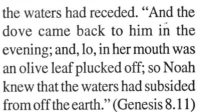ciliation with humanity through Noah. During the flood, Noah sent a dove from the ark to determine whether the waters had receded. "And the dove came back to him in the evening; and, lo, in her mouth was an olive leaf plucked off; so Noah knew that the waters had subsided from off the earth." (Genesis 8.11)

Om. The Creative Word; deemed to be that original sound, the generative first word or tone that vibrated through the receptive void, shaping and continuing to maintain creation. Also known as the great primordial sound, the sound current or silent sound – the sound of all sounds together. Pronounced home, without the h, and usually prolonged, Om is the first and foremost syllable of the ancient, sophisticated Sanskrit language. Used as a power tone, the Om invokes divine interaction. Sometimes spelled and pronounced Aum, the Om of the Vedas comes to us in the sacred word Hum of the Tibetans, the Amin of the Muslims, and the Amen of the Egyptians, Greeks, Romans, and Jews. In Hebrew it means "sure and faithful." Amen as used by Christians usually is translated "so it is" or "so be it." A more esoteric translation is "and so I affirm"–an active proclamation, not a passive agreement.

Om mani padme hum. A Buddhist chant, literally, "Hail, jewel in the lotus within. Amen." *Mani padme* represents the jewel of the lotus, the essential wisdom lying at the heart of Buddhist doctrine, the divine essence. *Hum* is the limitless reality embodied within the limits of the individual being, uniting the individual with the universal.

Om namah shivaya. "In the name of SHIVA" or "Lord, you are my very refuge." One of many mantras uttering god names. Any god or goddess name may be used: Allah, Brahma, Kali, Diana, whatever deity we would invoke for assistance and/or protection.

Omnipotence. All-powerful; having unlimited or universal power, authority, or force.

Omnipresent. Being present everywhere, with no limitation. The prefix is from the Latin *omnis,* meaning "all."

Omniscience. All-knowing, such as the mind of God.

"One becomes three." The truth held as a part of right formation that the one divine and only reality divides into male and female for manifestation in the outer world to occur. Kabalistically speaking, KETHER (the One) expresses itself through CHOKMAH (male) and BINAH (female). *See* "Three becomes seven" *and* "Seven becomes twelve."

Oral tradition. The ancient wisdom passed down through the spoken word which only recently has begun to appear in written

form, often having been distributed through stories, music,
poetry and drama, allegory and
myth.

Ordination. A sacrament of the
Christian tradition wherein the
devotee vows obedience to God
and the Christ. This ordained one
serves the church, community of
believers, and the world as a
spiritual guide and teacher.

Origen. b. Egypt, c. A.D. 185, d.
254. Alexandrian theologian,
teacher, and spiritual writer of the
early Christian church who led a
life of strict asceticism demanding
severe fasting, vigils, and poverty.
He believed the soul existed with
God prior to the creation of the
physical body, that the Genesis
stories of creation and the fall of
man were allegorical, not factual
accounts. He taught that all things
have a double aspect: corporeal and
sensible, accessible to all, and
spiritual and mystical, discerned
only by the enlightened. He
believed that suffering and pain are
part of God's redemptive plan and
that there is spiritual resurrection
for fallen souls. Imprisoned and
persecuted during his lifetime, he
was eventually condemned as a
heretic. Though often misunderstood or altered, his teachings stood
for 500 years before being

anathematized, and are now
reemerging. Origen's influence on
Christianity is considered to be
monumental. *Hexapla*; *De Prin-
cipiis*.

Orphic. Derived from *Orpheus,*
the poet and musician of Greek
mythology who is symbolic of the
most important mystery religions.
A person who seeks experiences
of God through the senses–as in
nature, music, art, drama, feeling,
etc. PANTHEISM is considered an
orphic approach to spirituality.

Ouija board. A tool for making
contact with the spirit world; a
"divining" board on which is
painted the alphabet and numbers
one through nine plus zero. Its
planchette, or pointer, easily
manipulated, moves from letter to
letter to spell answers to questions.
Since even a spirit of little
intelligence or lower consciousness may access, the inquirer may
be misled. The ouija is thus
considered a reckless method of
attempting communication.

Ouroborus. This cosmic serpent,
depicted with its tail in its mouth,
is the symbol of
the manifested
universe in its
cyclic aspect of
completeness.
The feathered

serpent of the Western wisdom tradition symbolizes the primordial unity that encloses all time and space. As the serpent encircles the all, it represents wisdom contained. In depth-psychology, it typifies the Earth, the Great Mother against whom evolving consciousness (in myth, the hero fighting the dragon or serpent) must struggle in order to individuate. Also the symbol of the RING-PASS-NOT and of the PLEROMA.

Outer planes. The so-called physical, astral (emotional), and mental planes of personality.

Out-of-body experience (OBE). A specific incident of becoming aware of oneself when consciousness is focused in the astral vehicle rather than the physical. Experiencers realize there is an awareness not attached to our physical body, and that we can continue to recognize and know without a physical body. This ASTRAL TRAVEL/projection relieves a great deal of anxiety concerning life's continuance after bodily death.

Overlighting. A method of the higher world to provide strength and awareness to a worker in the dense world. Overlighting fortifies the worker.

Overshadowing. An influence of the higher world coming into or over the receptive, sensitive disciple for the purpose of the higher reality. Done in such a way as to dignify humanity and serve Christ (called by whatever name), the overshadowing delivers energy, a message, or an influence of the Holy to humanity. Three ways are being exerted at this time to stimulate the flow of the CHRIST CONSCIOUSNESS to humanity:

1) overshadowing currently incarnated disciples and initiates;

2) pouring the Christ life or consciousness upon the masses;

3) his reappearance among humanity.

Oversoul. The blended group consciousness that occurs as the same individuals participate regularly in an action, i.e., family, group, team.

P

Pagan. From the Latin *paganus,* meaning a "country dweller." A practitioner of an Earth religion.

Palmistry. A study of the map or divine design contained in each hand that reveals influences at work and traits carried by the incarnated one. A study may thus disclose many insights into a person's life.

Pantheism. The belief that God, nature, and the universe are the same.

Paramahansa. *See* Swami.

Parapsychology. The emerging scientific study of PSI, ESP, and the psychic realities in order to more rationally understand the phenomena of altered states and dimensions previously little-understood, usually either feared or revered. *Para* means "beyond."

Parsee, or Parsi. A member of the ZOROASTRIAN sect in India, descended from Persians.

Passive meditation. The primary work of this gentle, open, and receptive procedure is to BUILD THE CUP mechanism needed to capture the droplets received for conscious comprehension – often a goal of first practices. Generally used to connect outer consciousness to the brain's RIGHT-HEMISPHERE capabilities. Ultimately this cup develops into the chalice into which the Living Fire will flow. *See* Active meditation.

Past life. Previous incarnation on the physical dimension.

Past-life regression. A technique to bring about an altered state of consciousness to guide us to review, study, and heal through recalling or re-experiencing past happenings in order to free us from the grip of present obstacles to growth and wholeness.

Patanjali. 3rd century A.D. Indian founder of the yoga system of Hindu philosophy. He defined the purpose of YOGA as knowledge of the true self. The four books of his *Yoga Sutra* set forth the moral and physical disciplines necessary to attain *moksha,* absolute freedom of self, as a result of gaining cosmic consciousness. *How to Know God: The Yoga Aphorisms of Patanjali,* trans. 1953.

Path of occultism. "The taking of heaven by storm" and intent, rather than comfortably awaiting advancement by evolution with our peers.

Path, the (of Initiation). The avenue taken by those seeking knowledge of the divine mysteries of life; the process of enlightenment through dedicated service and self-mastery, and the steps or stages delineated by various esoteric systems. As distinguished from the probationary path or the path of discipleship, a higher stage of spiritual evolution. Entrance upon the Path of Initiation is marked by simplification of the life, increased self-mastery, and conscious service to the divine Plan. Stages of development in which the center of

consciousness transfers from purely human awareness to early stages of spiritual awareness. Also, the pattern of advancement. In Christianity, the human Path of Initiation comprises five great steps as modeled by Master Jesus in his life: birth, baptism, transfiguration, crucifixion-resurrection, and ascension. Each step symbolizes a test we must pass and strengths we must embody to advance. Also, a way, a walk, or journey, usually depicting the spiritual story of our advancement.

Peacock. In the East the peacock is a symbol of the MASTER, the one who has experienced many lives through which to view the world (each feather contains an eye) and learn lessons. In medieval Christianity the peacock represented the Christ. At the Cathedral of Wells, England, a peacock with flowing tail sits as the Christ upon a large cross, a symbol somewhat like the phoenix rising from the ashes, a representation of the emergence of high consciousness.

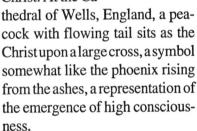

Pendulum. A tool used for divining. As a symbol, the shape of the swinging pendulum is a triangle, the two extreme ends coming to rest at center, held steady by a higher position (or view).

Pentecost. A festival of the Christian church commemorating the descent of the Holy Spirit to the apostles of Jesus, the Christ, in the physical world. Pentecost Sunday is the seventh Sunday after Easter, but the season extends to the last Sunday in August. These miraculous phenomena fulfilled Christ's promise not to leave unattended those he had left behind. The early disciples became connected and guided by this high consciousness, thus preparing them for their work to establish the KINGDOM OF SOULS on Earth. The color for Pentecost Sunday is red for the blood of Christian martyrs and for the fire of the Holy Spirit. The second Sunday of the season, Trinity Sunday, commemorates God as the Creator (Father-Mother), God the Son, and God the Holy Spirit; its color is white. The remainder of the season is red. From Acts 2 we learn about the tongues of fire in the symbol. The descending dove–Sophia/ Wisdom–is also used as a symbol of Pentecost.

Pentecostal. In Christianity, particular denominations emphasizing the GIFTS OF THE SPIRIT that manifested to the apostles on Pentecost Sunday. These denominations, in general, believe we must manifest one or more of the gifts as a sign of personal salvation. *See* Neo-Pentecostal.

Periodic abstinence. The practice of sexual self-discipline by choosing periods of abstinence from sexual activity for the purpose of self-control and lifting the focus of a relationship to a spiritual nature of interaction, rather than allowing the relationship to be maintained on the personality level. Most spiritual teachers recommend some practices of sexual control, and periodic abstinence is a discipline useful to most chelas.

Permanent atom. The atoms or small force centers around which the various bodies (physical, emotional, mental, and spiritual) of an individual are built and which the MONAD has appropriated for its purposes. These centers form the parts of the personality, each of which distributes a certain type of force and is able to respond to a particular vibration.

Personality. The physical, emotional, and lower-mental vehicles projected by the Soul into the denser planes through which it experiences life in the slower-vibrating realities for the purpose of learning and maturing.

Peshitta Bible. The Authorized Bible of the Church of the East. *Peshitta* means straight, simple, sincere, and true, i.e., the original. The name was given to this ancient and authoritative text to distinguish it from other Bible revisions and translations introduced into some of the Churches of the East (Monophysites) after the division at Ephesus and Chalcedon in A.D. 431 and 451, respectively. Because this text was in use 400 years before the Christian Church was divided into several sects, it remains the only authoritative text of the Old and New Testaments of all Eastern Christians in the Near East and India, the Church of the East, the Roman Catholic Church in the East, the Monophysites, and Indian Christians. However, since all Christians, even the Moslems, in the Middle East accept and revere the Peshitta text, it proves beyond a doubt that it was in use many centuries before the division of the Church. [Reprinted from *The Holy Bible from Ancient Eastern Manuscripts,* by George M. Lamsa (Philadelphia: A. J. Holman Co., 1933).]

Phenomenon. In esoteric thought, an experience or happening not definable or explainable by the laws of physical science.

Philia. The Greek word meaning friendship, personal affection, or fondness; love of friends or our fellow beings; familial love of tribe or family. Social sympathy, but not unconditional, as is empathy.

Philosopher's Stone. Energies, concepts, and realizations synthesized and concretized by those on the path of rapid ascent, used to evaluate life experiences. The finding of this stone or substance was the goal of ALCHEMY practiced in the Middle Ages. It was believed that a small tincture of it would transmute large amounts of base metals into gold, heal deadly wounds, and completely transform the body and soul of the alchemist who achieved its manufacture. The stone is thought to be an allegorical interpretation of the highest states of mystical awareness attained by the alchemists as they projected their own personal transmutation process onto their chemical experiments or procedures. Although the actual relationship between consciousness and matter is still a scientific uncertainty, in esoteric and mystical circles it is generally accepted that matter is just a lower vibration of spiritual modalities, therefore subject to transmutation.

Phoenix. A mythological bird of Egypt used as a symbol for resurrection and rebirth. The phoenix is said to rise from its own ashes every five hundred years, to re-form more refined and beautiful. Often used to symbolize truth and hope for civilizations and particular faiths.

Phylactery. Two small leather boxes containing strips of parchment inscribed with quotations from the Hebrew scriptures which are used by Jewish men during morning worship. It invokes physical action, repetitive prayer, and the holding of thoughts in contemplation/meditation.

Pierce the veil. To break through the boundaries of rational thought and penetrate higher collective wisdom, often called the CLOUD OF KNOWABLE THINGS or the MIND OF GOD.

Pineal gland. Believed to be the endocrine gland into which the energy of the brow center flows–in effect, the home of the THIRD EYE.

Pingala. One part of a threefold current, or channel, through which the KUNDALINI rises along the spinal column from the base of the spine to the crown center. The current on the right is the pingala and is associated with the masculine stream of energy, or the force side, of this three-part body mechanism. *See* Sushumna; Ida.

Piscean Age. A cycle of time wherein the Earth received the influence of the constellation Pisces, according to astronomy and astrology; roughly calculated from about the time of Master Jesus' birth until 1987.

Pituitary gland. Believed to be the endocrine gland into which the energy of the crown center flows; in effect, the point of contact for the soul wherein it is anchored into the physical, mechanical form.

Plan. The blueprint of evolution, as made known through the ELDER BROTHERS of Humanity. The divine Plan represents God's design for humanity, for the planet, and for all life. Knowledge of this Plan will guide humanity back to the Source of life and enable us to become conscious coworkers. Considered a MANDALA of action projected to humanity to aid us in finding our way home. A manifestation of divine law; the order and purpose that prevails throughout all existence.

Planes: physical, emotional, mental, intuitional, atmic, monadic, divine. A gathering of similar vibrations and natures into defined frequencies. Each plane consists of seven levels and is delineated gradually as the denser planes form a layer and the less dense build upon it until seven substrata are formed.

Planes, cosmic. Usually a reference to only the higher planes of the soul and monad (intuitional, atmic, MONADIC, and divine) or to only the highest-vibrating level of each of the seven planes, i.e., physical, reflecting (etheric) ether. Some teachers delineate the soul in its world of intuitive and atmic planes and the monad in its arena of monadic and divine.

Planetary body. Humanity, as a group of cells within planet Earth; spiritual teachings suggest humanity forms the cerebro-spinal nature of our planet.

Planetary chain. The lives of a planet linked in a series. Seven incarnations exist in a chain–descending: mental, astral, etheric, physical; ascending: etheric, astral, mental.

Planetary Christ. The Christ, head of HIERARCHY, who reigns supreme over the planet and its Hierarchy, angels, and humanity; the guiding consciousness of the planet.

Planetary Logos. The indwelling High Consciousness that has formed the planet as a physical body for the purpose of evolving consciousness, both its own and that of the little lives on it and in it.

Planetary spirit. The vital essence (not form) energizing the life of the planet.

Planetary workers. Those whose allegiance is pledged to the advancement of the goals of the planet collectively and in obedience to the planetary Logos.

Planets. *See pages 143-144.*

Pleroma. In Greek, "fullness." The supreme divinity in GNOSTICISM. The uncorrupted world of divine perfection, the abode of the invisible gods, space developed and divided, the divine world, or universal soul. Because the Pleroma includes all things, the drama of the fall of SOPHIA and the creation of the world by the DEMIURGE take place in it.

Podvig. An Agni term. Not translatable from Russian, but implying a great or heroic deed; spiritual achievement that unites the soul in greater expression in the life.

Planets
and their astrological impact

Earth. Our home planet is considered a non-sacred planet in process of transformation, preparing for an INITIATION. Located in the horoscope directly across from the SUN, we write the Earth into our charts and study its influence somewhat with the aid of ESOTERIC ASTROLOGY. It is considered to be RAY 2 in nature; however, humanity is expressing collectively on Ray 4 which helps the blending of personality and soul.

Jupiter. The placement of this planet indicates areas of good fortune, growth, and expansion in life. Known as a spiritual planet, Jupiter often signals areas of spiritual expression or fervor. The ruler of the sign of Sagittarius, it is considered Ray 2 in nature.

Mars. The planet that symbolizes the type and amount of physical strength and stamina we have by birthright. This planet asseerts the masculine side of our nature, and where we will expend physical effort. The ruler of Aries, it is considered Ray 6 in nature.

Mercury. The planet of communication and mental capabilities. ASPECTS to Mercury help us understand our mental makeup, how our minds work, and what we enjoy studying or contemplating. The ruler of the signs of Gemini and Virgo, it is considered Ray 4 in nature.

Moon. This indicator of the astral nature and subconscious pattern we hold within the subtler part of our natures is revealed through our emotions. Placement of the Moon determines areas of great attachment or passion, so success here is very satisfying. The importance of the Moon in interpreting a personal horoscope is second only to the Sun. The Moon rules the sign of Cancer and is considered Ray 4 in nature.

Planets and their astrological impact (continued)

Neptune. The planet that indicates spiritual expression. Its placement in a horoscope reveals where we must face illusion or delusion. A well-aspected Neptune can help us with active creativity and imagination, usually after we have elevated our spiritual understanding. Ruler of Pisces, it is considered Ray 6 in nature.

Pluto. This planet is the indicator of rejuvenation and power. Its location becomes a place of challenge for our use of will and personal power. The newest planet, Pluto often indicates where we could be secretive or less comfortable being direct about matters. Often seen as the planet of the underworld or subconscious. Ruler of Scorpio, it is considered Ray 1 in nature.

Saturn. The planet of discipline, structure, and responsibility, Saturn's placement indicates areas of restriction, self-induced or otherwise. Known as the teacher, or angel of discipline, Saturn conveys the lessons of life; here we make progress as we earn it–usually slowly. Ruler of Capricorn, it is considered Ray 3 in nature.

Sun. The major focus of the personal horoscope representing our life force, will, and inner life. Its location indicates the character being developed and refined, as well as the life thrust. The Sun governs the physical heart and personal stamina. The Sun rules the sign of Leo and is considered Ray 2 in nature.

Uranus. The planet of rapid change and great daring, the placement of Uranus in a horoscope suggests where we might be revolutionary or futuristic in our thinking or behavior. Here freedom is experienced, and creativity runs high. Ruler of the sign of Aquarius, it is considered Ray 7 in nature.

Venus. The planet of beauty and love. In a horoscope the aspects to Venus are important indications of the manner in which we express our passion for life, and the placement will reveal the kinds of things we will love. Venus represents the feminine nature as well. The ruler of the signs of Taurus and Libra, it is considered Ray 5 in nature.

See Astrology.

Polarity (Hermetic principle of). The belief that everything is reflected by opposites; poles of opposites hold the line of tension upon which all life advances in the dual world. Polarities range from black or white, female or male, give or receive, express or stifle, fire or water, inhale or exhale, empty or full, and to create or destroy.

Polarity therapy. A healing technique to balance points in the etheric body.

Political organizers. A category of WORLD SERVERS who work through integrated head, heart, and root CHAKRAS to step down the higher PLAN for humanity.

Politics. The art of people living and working together for the fulfillment of group needs.

Portal of initiation. Doorway to the testing experience.

Possession. In spiritual thought a condition in which the soul which has created a personality is blocked by a possessing entity, which, having taken command, blocks the creator's goals and substitutes its own. A negative condition with SPIRIT RELEASEMENT needed to return the personality life to order.

Poverty. A vow often taken by a subordinate of a spiritual order in return for initiation or admittance into a particular tradition. The idea is twofold: that all that one has belongs equally to all others of the order, and that all one truly owns is what is contained in the soul. Such reasoning is to teach that outer things are for right use in the world and do not belong in the truest sense in the real world, but are only the trappings of the material plane.

Power words. Words carrying a particularly high charge of energy into and/or through the consciousness of the speaker for a personal or group purpose. Such words selected for their effect are used by knowledgeable ones to direct energy for specific reasons. Common and beneficial power words are OM, K'IN, SHALOM, MIR, Amen, SHANTI, HO.

Powers. Angels of an advanced order who work under the LORDS OF KARMA to balance good and evil in human lives and in planetary systems. Powers deal with the universal law of cause and effect and work to transmute evil to good through strength, severity, fortitude, and justice.

Practitioner. Specifically at Sancta Sophia Seminary located at the intentional spiritual community of Sparrow Hawk Village, Tahlequah, Oklahoma, one who has completed foundation work and demonstrated integrity, earning the endorsement of the religious society.

Pralaya. A period of unmanifest when the second and third aspects of the trinity rest in the first before a renewed cycle begins. A Sanskrit word meaning "period of dissolution or destruction." In Hindu philosophy, the end of the world; also called "Night of Brahma."

Prana. The Sanskrit word for breath. In mystic and occult philosophy the vital air, the life principle. The psycho-electrical field that manifests in the individual as vitality. The life-atoms of the prana, or psycho-electrical field, return to natural pranic reservoirs of the planet at the time of death. Also known as *ki* or *chi,* prana is the cosmic life force on all planes of being; the "breath of life."

Pratyeka-Buddhas. Meaning "Buddhahood for self alone." Those who have passed beyond the wheel of rebirth and the material world and returned to its origin, the divine source. As the cause for rebirth is eliminated, so is the ability to exercise compassion no longer available. The path of the Pratyeka-Buddha leads to immediate real-ization of the goal (bliss) and is called the "open path."

Prayer. The deliberate attempt to center ourselves in conversation with God or deity of choice; the concentration of heart and mind that brings that communion. The message sent to the Creator through conscious and unconscious wishes, thoughts, and aspirations, representing our search to fulfill our needs and to stretch beyond ourselves to a greater identity and a clear awareness of God's presence in our lives. Often simplified as "our talking to God," while meditation represents "our listening for God."

Prayer wheel. A spiritual tool of the Buddhist tradition wherein a container with many prayers in it is spun while in a prayerful state of mind, activating the prayers within for a time and for the intention of the one praying.

Predestination. A dogma that denies free will, believing all experiences are foreordained by God with little to no chance of change –"a train on a track with no switches." The concept denies humans the ability to make creative changes. We are relegated to either salvation or damnation.

Pre-existence. A teaching of the soul's discarnate existence with God prior to the creation of the body. ORIGEN's work was anathematized by his strong stand on pre-existence, not REINCARNATION as popularly believed.

Principalities (also known as Princedoms). Angels of an advanced order who are in charge of group minds and nations. Serving as the angelic rulers of the nations of the world, they are associated with firmness and victory.

Principle of Directed Purpose. Humanity is directed by the NIRMANAKAYAS and the Group of WORLD SERVERS to learn to relate to one another. Through 1) synthesis, 2) focused intention, and 3) right use of will, they 4) direct energy to one another, thereby strengthening life within form.

Probationary path. A time before acceptance into the initiatory process when we are closely guided, tested, and evaluated for eligibility for conscious evolution.

Prometheus. A Titan in Greek mythology who survived the fall of Atlantis and was a friend to humanity. Chosen to arbitrate apportionment of a slaughtered bull, Prometheus tricked Zeus into taking the bones and fat (which thereafter always remained the gods' portion) and leaving the meat for humanity. An angered Zeus withheld fire from humanity so that the meat would have to be eaten raw. When Prometheus, aided by Athene, stole fire from the chariot of the Sun and gave it to humanity, Zeus punished him by chaining him to a pillar in the Caucasian Mountains. Each day a vulture came and ate out his liver; and each night the liver grew back, only to be eaten again. Prometheus is a symbol of the consequences incurred when humanity evolved into Self-consciousness (the fire of the Gods emits the light of consciousness). No longer in blissful preconscious slumber, humanity is now chained (by its own awareness) to the rock of materiality and must constantly undergo pains of purification (the liver is the organ of purification) in order to remain worthy of the inner fiery presence.

Prophecy. The foretelling of a possible occurence or the reading of a projected outcome if actions continue as they are. Future events are changeable, so prophecies may be taken as warnings and adjustments made to life, if necessary.

Psi. The entire field of phenomena generally known as PARAPSYCHOLOGY.

Psyche. The spirit, or soul, as distinguished from the physical form. From the Greek word *psyche* meaning soul, self, or mind.

Psychic art. Renderings guided by psychic attunement.

Psychic development. The enhancing of natural abilities of perception and extended sense awareness through practice and opening the mind to new understanding.

Psychic reading. Using psychic senses, an attunement is made to an individual or situation for the purpose of receiving and gathering impressions. This contact may be initiated by numerous means.

Psychic residue. An Agni Yoga term. That which the psyche carries from the imprint of experience, e.g., child abuse, traumatic divorce, a fire – even after the experience itself has been evaluated and its lesson gleaned. The resulting residual must then be purified in the light of the soul. Remnants can be given proper PURIFICATION by intent.

Psychic senses. The nonphysical sensory mechanism of the nonphysical nature, also known as extended sense awareness, GIFTS OF THE SPIRIT, and by particular names, i.e., CLAIRVOYANCE, CLAIRSENTIENCE, CLAIRAUDIENCE, etc.

Psychic surgery. A particularly hard-to-understand technique of using spiritual/psychic energy to permeate matter (the body) to initiate change, corrections, and removal of physical difficulties.

Psychism. The practice or exercise of extrasensory awareness; sensitivity to nonphysical or unseen forces, allowing for heightened perception and understanding. A capacity of the mind or soul as distinguished from the physical and psychological aspect of an individual; a natural ability that allows conscious awareness of the realities and activities of more subtle planes. This may be positive or negative, according to purpose and intent or level of awareness being exercised. Ethical use of psychism does not violate the freedom or will of others.

Psychism, negative. The use of extrasensory awareness in a materialistic manner, working from the lower chakras or self-interest.

Psychism, positive. The appropriate use of spiritual senses to assist an awareness of the nature of life and in service to humanity and the higher Plan.

Psychography. Mapping or graphing the forces of the soul–including past, present, and future lives–that affect the present life and personality.

Psychokinesis (PK). Moving physical articles by the power of mind; the use of mind power by paranormal abilities. Uri Geller has demonstrated such abilities in the 20th century under the scrutiny of trained observers.

Psychologists. A category of WORLD SERVERS who work through integrated head, heart, solar plexus, and throat chakras to step down the higher PLAN for humanity. Also, a recognized professional involved with the interfacing of personality and soul.

Psychometry. A technique of holding an object and attuning to a previous owner or using the object as a point of focus for gathering information through the psychic senses, primarily that of touch.

Psychospiritual. The mental effort made to prepare the mind and mental body to embrace the spiritual level (soul) in preparation for soul infusion.

Psychosynthesis. A counseling technique developed by ROBERTO ASSAGIOLI to assist spiritual growth through acknowledging the soul and developing will and wisdom.

Purgatory. This term refers to the purging of distortions that must be experienced on the journey to high consciousness. In *Opening to Inner Light,* author Ralph Metzner says wisely: HEAVEN is the wonderful experience wherein we know we are one with all life, purgatory is the journey of the soul through life and to maturity, and hell is when we get stuck.

Purification. The cleansing and clearing of distortions or impurities. Meditation and spiritual techniques can heal, mend, or cleanse our astral and mental ethers of psychic residue that obscures higher consciousness. Spiritual disciplines and psychological techniques that dissolve barriers to awareness are for this purpose.

Purity. Agni virtue for Virgo. A state of mind, purity is best understood by thinking of clarity. Level by level we purify the personality of its distortions, glamours, and illusions. Cleanliness of body, purity of heart, and clarity of mind are gained by persistent observation and holding oneself in the light of the soul.

Purpose. The intentional nature of all activity–cosmic, planetary, human, or microscopic. The fire of divine impulse that permeates and motivates all forms toward certain action and achievement; the originating cause. The operating and intelligent will guiding every living thing along destined paths.

Pyramid. One of the shapes of SA-CRED GEOMETRY. Four triangular-shaped sides fit together. The number 4 symbolizes the material foundation and the three-sided triangle represents the TRINITY. Together they create 4x3=12, a number that reduces to 3, returning us to the trinity–at work as the number of perfected order of trinity made manifest. A part of the formula of creation: ONE BECOMES THREE BE-COMES SEVEN BECOMES TWELVE, reflecting the inner plan on the Earth plane. *See* Numerology.

Pythagoras. b. Samos, n.d., d. 497 B.C. Greek philosopher, sage, and mathematician. He established a religious community in southern Italy of which little is known. He wrote nothing, and his whole life is cloaked in myth and legend. Pythagoreanism was a way of life (rather than a philosophy) based on asceticism and purification, the relatedness of all living things, rules of abstinence, and beliefs about the understanding and representation of the world of nature through numbers. It propounded that number is the essence of all things and the principle of rational order in the universe. Its leading theological doctrine was METEM-PSYCHOSIS, the doctrine that souls migrate from one body to another until complete purification is achieved. Pythagoras believed all spiritual students trained to live lives of profound service must also study either mathematics or physical science to maintain balanced consciousness as they expand their awareness into other dimensions.

Q

Quatrefoil. This design consisting of four lobes or foils of equal size represents the four evangelists: Matthew, Mark, Luke, and John. Now sometimes used to symbolize the cornerstones of church unity: scriptures, creed, sacraments, and orders.

Quetzalcoatl. Best-known name for the feathered serpent in the Mesoamerican traditions (others are *Kukulcan* in the Yucatan and *Gucumatz* in the more southern countries). The *quetzal* is a rare, brilliantly colored green bird found only in the highlands of South America, and *coatl* means serpent; thus, "feathered serpent." Also, *co* (serpent) is combined with *atl* (water) to mean literally "feathered serpent of the water." Thus we have the serpent (wisdom) that has evolved out of the water of life (the collective unconscious) and evolved to fly (high consciousness, the feathers of the crown unfolded). *See* Ouroborus.

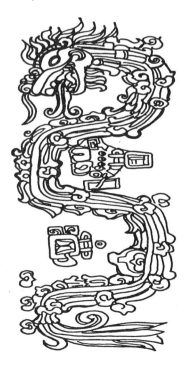

R

Race of men. As used in esoteric teachings and the GREAT INVOCATION, "men" derives from *manas,* a Sanskrit term meaning "to think." The term refers to the kingdom of humanity that evolved from the animal kingdom to become the mind-beings whose thought capability was to build the mental plane for the planet and to supply the mechanism whose thoughts or focus would create the circumstances to manifest in planetary life. Ultimately the mind of humanity is to harmonize with the Mind of God and thus resolve disharmony.

Radionics. A healing method facilitated through an instrument or device using the ESP faculty. A trained, capable practitioner can discover the cause of disease–human, animal, plant, soil – through a series of questions and answers believed to use the extra intelligence of the collective that each person has touched. Usually a technique for working at a distance.

Rainbow bridge. A common name for the ANTAHKARANA. Also associated with a specific technique to hasten the development of the antahkarana through spiritual focus.

Raja Yoga. *See* Yoga.

Rajas. The central one of three GUNAS, the electric qualities influencing all of life. The neutralizing influence of restlessness, rajas is compulsive – activity for the sake of motion; also known as rhythm (harmony).

Rays, the seven. *See page 154.*

Reappearance of the Christ. In esoteric Christianity, the re-emergence of the Christ, who said, "Lo, I will be with you even until

Seven Rays

Ray. One of seven streams of force, or emanations, from the Logos; the seven qualities of God expressing individualized attributes of divine nature. Each bequeaths its quality, color, and sound as it impacts consciousness. The seven Rays are divided into three major Rays of aspect and four minor Rays of attribute. The Rulers, or Chohans, of the Rays are also known as Seven Spirits, or ELDER BROTHERS BEFORE THE THRONE, or (in Eastern thought) Seven Great RISHIS.

Rays of Aspect

Ray 1 – Will, or Power
Red. Each Age is ushered in with a flood of Ray 1 energy. Relates to politicians, those learning to use will, the science of true statesmanship/government, and those learning the technique of manifesting money. The strong influence of Ray 1 creates the initiator-type with leadership abilities.

Ray 2 – Love-Wisdom
Blue. Relates to the science of meditation and social evolution, psychology, all sciences of initiation. These sciences produce the true psychic. The strong influence of Ray 2 creates a maintainer-type with teaching and healing abilities.

Ray 3 – Active Intelligence, Adapability
Yellow. Relates to the history of EVOLUTION, laws governing humanity, OCCULT use of money, the science of communication with spiritual Cloud of Knowable Things. The strong influence of Ray 3 creates a mediator type with a philosophical nature.

Rays of Attribute

Ray 4 – Harmony through Conflict to Unity
Green. Relates to the science of color and sound, study of ETHERIC BODY, science of crisis, tension, and new emergence. The true artist surfaces.

Ray 5 – Concrete Knowledge, Exactness
Orange. Relates to the study of life and space, awareness of energies, laws of the cosmos, and hidden chemistry, the science of the soul, meditation, and right use of mind. Unlocking science of electricity and esoteric healing.

Ray 6 – Abstract Idealism, Devotion
Indigo or rose. Relates to the science of approaches to the Higher, the mysteries of INITIATION, the science of service. New awareness of the unseen world emerges.

Ray 7 – Ceremonial Magic, or Law of Economy
Purple. Relates to the science of cycles, soul and personality, order and orderliness, divine simplicity, ceremonial magic, and finance.

the end," is the fulfilling of a commitment to humanity. The Christ is not returning for he has not left humanity; he or she is expected to reappear in the near future, but no one knows the day or the hour.

Rebirthing. A gentle, safe breathing process that releases accumulated negativity, from the present, back to and including the birth process. Unwanted behavior patterns are uncovered and let go, opening the heart center for more love, peace, and abundance. A powerful healing tool.

Recapitulation. To recall, repeat, or re-experience. In each life the human species is said to recapitulate the evolution of humanity from "frog" level to fetus to baby. In spiritual thought we recapitulate our experiences of previous incarnations to reach a level of knowing more quickly so that we can again step forth and advance on a path of new learning. Recapitulation moves rapidly compared to new growth which proceeds more deliberately.

Redemption. The process of reclaiming or recovering our identity with the Source of all creation and becoming all we have truly been from the beginning. The return of all aspects of life into harmonious union with God through awakening the divine spark, or spiritual aspect, latent within matter. In the deliverance of humanity from the world of appearances, spirituality realigns us to the world of spirit, enabling our recognition of our divine nature.

Reflected world. A mirror image of the real cast upon the dense ethers – appearing as authentic, though actually illusory. Contains reflections of the meaning of nature and the thoughts and acts of humanity. A temporary reality – not eternal. The world of MAYA.

Reflective ethers. The subtle ethers of the less dense planes that easily absorb impressions. Such ethers exist in the etheric level of the physical body and plane, as well as the astral. Here a history of experience is chronicled as a living story called the AKASHIC RECORD.

Reflexology. A spiritual healing technique applying pressure upon specific points of the feet (or hands) of a patient to balance and distribute energy throughout the physical body. Each organ and system of the human body has a reference point in the feet, the hands, the ears, the tongue, and the face.

Regression. Returning to an earlier point of consciousness. *See* Past-life regression.

Reiki therapy. *Reiki* is the Japanese word for "universal life energy." *Rei* describes the universal part of the energy – the spirit, or soul, which is continually creating–and *ki* is actually a part of that *rei* force, indicating the energy which flows through all living things. "Reiki," as it is commonly used, refers to the Usui System of Natural Healing. After a practitioner has been opened to become a reiki channel for the energy, the energy force flows through the hands when they are placed upon oneself, another person, an animal, plant, or anything. Through the use of ancient symbols, it can flow anywhere. The energy seems to have an intelligence of its own, for when the therapist is working with another, the reiki energy will flow to the area where it is needed most, no matter where the hands are placed. Rediscovered by Dr. Mikao Usui late in the 19th century, and brought to the United States by Mrs. Hawayo Takote in the 1970s.

Reincarnation. A teaching based upon the combination of the doctrine of the perfectibility of humanity and the principle of periodicity. The human, essentially of a spiritual nature, comes as a seed of Deity into the superphysical and physical worlds to develop into a perfected human being. As such achievement is rarely possible in one Earthlife, for neither time nor opportunity exists to develop every human power, the principle of periodicity–ebb and flow, going forth and returning–provides each human with opportunities and activities to enter physical incarnation, to experience variations of race, gender, caste, and environment. On the ascending spiral path by which we reach our goal of adeptship, each cycle consists of a descent of a portion of the power, life, and consciousness of the ego into physical incarnation and a subsequent return to the nonphysical through which the soul matures in consciousness toward wisdom.

Religion. A system of dogma and creeds used to guide the outer life in expression of belief in a supernatural power. Religion forms a specific pattern or dogma–the way experienced, given, received, and lived by prophets or inspired ones–followed by others to aid in spiritual growth.

"Remember to remember." A Maya expression of great importance in this time of transition between ages, particularly 1987 through 2012, as inner awareness and outer knowledge are reconnecting.

Reptilian brain. The earliest developed brain that formed the mechanical know-how of the physical form and exists to serve, correct, and heal the body itself.

"Resist not evil." Matthew 5.39 (KJV) Do not engage your energy with acts considered against evil or against the flow of evolution. Save your strength for doing good. Buddha as well said, "It is not enough to cease to do evil, it is time to do good."

Ѽ Responsibility. An Agni theme. We are charged to create a response to the experience of life – appropriate to our level of understanding and spirituality. We are empowered for the purpose of creating an appropriate response to the experience of life and the lessons it brings. Correlates to the energy and influence of the number 8.

Resurrection. The passage from the death of selfishness and individualism into a life of light, unity, and unselfish love; the state of being wholly identified with God. The realization of the divine whole of which each of us is a part and through which each is born into life eternal.

Revelations. Messages from spirit realities that link spiritual realities and human realities, including DREAMS, visitations, precognitive experiences, and psychic experiences.

Reverence. Agni virtue for Libra. Ѽ A more modern term for solemnity – a respect and appreciation of all life and an inner awareness of self-worth. Reverence values each aspect of life, granting dignity and awe to every revelation of the holy.

Rhythm (Hermetic principle of). "Everything flows out and in; everything has its tides; all things rise and fall; the pendulum-swing manifests in everything; the measure of the swing to the right is the measure of the swing to the left; rhythm compensates." *The Kybalion.*

Richards, Mira. b. France, 1878, d. 1973. Colleague of AUROBINDO, whom he called "THE MOTHER." She helped establish Auroville Ashram in Pondicherry, India, based on his concepts, which was to be a model of planetary consciousness "where human beings of good will could live freely as citizens and obey the single authority of Truth; a place of peace, concord and harmony where all the fighting instincts of man would be used exclusively to conquer the cause of his sufferings and miseries." Auroville remains incomplete.

157

Right-action. A spiritual term used to denote alignment with purpose.

Right-hand path. The mystical ascent upon the path which leads back to God. *See* Left-hand path; Evolution.

Right hemisphere (of brain). One part of the neocortex (the third brain) with unique characteristics, such as relating to the whole of life, bonding, accessing altered states, and the mammalian brain capabilities. *See* Three-brain concept.

Right-relationship. Self-explanatory but oft-used term in spiritual teachings for harmony between individuals, kingdoms, and perspectives, in accord with the higher purpose of life itself. An outmoded usage would be "righteousness."

Rig Veda. The most ancient of sacred verse, or teachings, of the Hindu tradition.

Ring-pass-not. The "barrier" between each plane of existence preventing ascent. The periphery of the sphere of influence of any life force from the tiny atom of matter to the great atom of a solar system. The limit of the field of activity of any center of positive life. While this confining barrier separates a living system from that which is outside that system, it is not a hindrance or limitation as we progress in evolution and consciousness expands. As consciousness is freed of restriction and vibrates to high realities, we pass easily through the ring into the next dimension. That which cannot vibrate faster or higher must be released for consciousness to continue its ascent.

Risen Christ. The Christ of Easter morning who demonstrated mastery over death.

Rishi. A Buddhist term for a wise or holy one, a saint or sage.

Ritual. A prescribed form or order of conducting sacred ceremonies or formulas used to invoke or evoke energies or emotions to empower life. With the RAY 7 influence increasing as we enter the AQUARIAN AGE, we will see a return of orderliness, less wasted emotion, energy, and effort. Rituals, formulas, and ceremonies serve us daily with little recognition. Daily rituals can easily slip below the level of consciousness and assist and empower individuals without recognition. In the new era we will bring to consciousness these formulas with greater understanding of their purpose and benefit.

Roerich, Helena. b. Russia, 1879, d. 1949. Feminist, educator, spiritualist, writer, and student of theosophy, whose books are today read throughout the world. She revealed that as a frail and sickly child she was frequently visited by MASTER MORYA who subsequently dictated to her the ancient wisdom teachings, particularly AGNI YOGA, the yoga of fire, in thirteen volumes. She predicted in her writings that the new epoch "under the Rays of Uranus will bring a renaissance of women; the Epoch of Maitreya is the Epoch of the Mother of the World." *Letters of Helena Roerich, Volumes I and II; On Eastern Crossroads; Foundations of Buddhism.*

Roerich, Nicholas. b. Russia, 1874, d. 1947. Visionary, author, artist, and New Age cultural leader. Husband of spiritualist writer Helena Roerich. His paintings have been called "unparalleled fiery, luminous, incandescent embodiments of the teachings of the Far East." Psychics said of him that, though old and white-bearded, he seemed to have "an aura of rosy, golden light about him." Writing, painting, and teaching in the early years of this century, the Roerichs believed humanity was entering upon a new era of human advancement when science, philosophy, religion, and culture would be taught as one, giving rise to an enlightened society resting upon the "cornerstone of knowledge and beauty." He foresaw in the new era an artistic return to religious themes since the dominant theme of an ancient culture was always expressed in its religion. He taught that the art of all nations must be protected and used as a transforming agent in our lives. Master Morya, Helena Roerich's spiritual mentor, said of Nicholas, "He is the true Agni Yogi. The fiery man stands for unity, for one humanity, linking the vision of the ages with the labor of daily life." *Shamballa,* 1930; *Realm of Light,* 1931; *Fiery Stronghold,* 1933.

Rolfing. A bodywork technique developed by Ida Rolf in the 1970s wherein she proved by freeing the fascia of the muscles the body could be manipulated and rebalanced in such a way that psychological shifts would follow. She addressed the memories held in the cells and set into motion a new wave of understanding concerning the body and its relationship to the psychological self.

Root race. In esoteric terminology seven stages of humanity–a series of group minds–develop during the cycle of planetary existence. As Earth's humanity passes through these seven root races, the human lifestream evolves. These progressive epochs of dominant cultural complexes, or peoples, are centered in geographic areas where the stream of divine sparks converges into expression–a root race. According to esoteric tradition, the seven primary groups in order are Adamic, Hyperborean (the first two groups, or races, did not take physical form), Lemurian, Atlantean, Aryan–the American-European group mind (also called Aryan) is the fifth sub-race, or the fifth part of the fifth root race in esoteric determination. Two are yet to emerge (the sixth has been named Aurorean). Each root race contains seven sub-races, which are like waves coming upon a shore, each evolving toward the goal of the root race in its cycle. Each root race–divided into seven periods, or sub-races–attains to a climax of achievement about its midpoint, the 4th sub-race. Here a racial cataclysm begins while a new race is born of the fifth sub-race of the root race in decline. The new root race then evolves with the latter half of the preceding mother race.

Rosary. A Christian tradition of prayers said while fingering strands of beads as specifically designated. Similar beads exist in other traditions for comparable purposes. In the East they are called MALA BEADS.

Rose. The rose has been used to represent prophecy and the chakras since the 13th century. "The  desert shall rejoice and blossom as a rose." (Isaiah 35.1) In most Western art–often placed upon a cross as in Rosicrucian or esoteric Christian traditions–the rose is as the lotus to the East, symbol of the soul.

Rosicrucianism. A philosophy of esoteric thought that claims its heritage back to a German Lutheran minister, Johan Valentin Andrea, in the early 16th century. A combination of esoteric Christianity and mystery school teachings from which emerged Freemasonry and early theosophy.

Runes. Stones used by the Vikings for divination. Many belief systems use stones in random techniques to guide the consciousness of the seer.

S

Sabbat. One of the seasonal festivals equally spaced during the year, celebrated by most neo-pagans and covens of witches.

Sabian symbols. A set of 360 symbols associated with a specific degree of astrological designation. The modern designations were created by Marc Edmund Jones through the ATTUNEMENT of Elsie Wheeler in 1925. Each degree has a specific picture or symbol assigned as a power point to be contemplated. Sabian was the name of Jones's school, and he gave the name to the system of symbols he originated. The concept of a symbol per degree was not new to Jones. It is believed that the Egyptians and the Chinese may have used the concept in an earlier period.

Sacraments. Sacred rituals or rites used to invoke spiritual force or power into individual lives and situations. Used as an energy of renewal, revitalization, or resurrection to the life, lifting it in potency and awareness. The seven sacraments of Esoteric Christianity are 1) Baptism, 2) Confession, 3) Confirmation, 4) Marriage, 5) Holy Orders, 6) Eucharist, or Communion, 7) Healing, formerly called Last Rites, the anointing of the sick and dying. *See individual listings.*

Sacred geometry. The way the essential creative mystery of God is rendered visible–the most cogent expression of the divine Plan known to humanity. A combination of ratios and proportions is the metaphysical pattern or blueprint underlying all manifested forms, e.g., from realms of thought, to universes, to solar systems, to human beings, to atoms. This repeating pattern of harmonic ratios and proportions is the esoteric structure which links MICROCOSMS to MACROCOSMS and allows OCCULT manifestation, according to the Hermetic law of correspondence, "as above, so below."

Sacred mysteries. *See* Mystery teachings.

Sacred space. An area properly prepared, constructed, and dedicated to spiritual work or purpose, often following designated formulas.

Sacrifice. Making sacred every aspect of life; sanctification brought about by the fire of purification as it consumes all that is not of the true self. From the Latin word *sacer,* meaning "sacred" and *facere,* meaning "to make." A sacred place is a safe place, dedicated, and set apart.

Sai Baba. A saint of India of the highest spiritual eminence who it is believed has reincarnated twice in this century. Though eccentric and flamboyant in his last incarnation (d. 1918), he is worshipped by his devotees as a Hindu God who is "always in the all-knowing state, always in a state of universal soul." He left many wondrous teachings to edify and enlighten, particularly that divine knowledge is to be realized, not taught, that the "unlearned state" which Taoism extols means not mere ignorance, but simplicity and integrity. It is not incompatible with learning; but learning cannot produce it, and absorption in learning can destroy it. Ignorance conceals pre-existent knowledge, "just as water plants cover the surface of a pond." The illusion that supposes phenomena are real is the screen of ignorance which hides knowledge. Tear it off and knowledge (Brahma) will shine forth. Sai Baba was said to sometimes have a wild manner, throwing stones at unwanted visitors, but the wealth heaped upon him daily, he disbursed daily; the sick were healed, the childless found families, and the doubting became the faithful. He said, "I give people what they want in the hope that they will begin to want what I want to give them." And, to those who needed to be near him, "I am with you whenever you think of me." *Sai Baba's Charters and Sayings* (published without copyright by All India Sai Samaj); Biography by Arthur Osborne: *The Incredible Sai Baba,* 1958.

Saint. One who has realized a high degree of spirituality, who hungers and thirsts for God; also one acknowledged and so designated by the Christian (Catholic) church through formal recognition.

Saint Augustine. b. Tagaste, North Africa, A.D. 354, d. A.D. 430. Perhaps the most influential theologian in the entire history of Western Christianity. After a dissolute, irresponsible youth, Augustine became a Christian and retired from the world to a monastic community devoted to prayer and contemplation. His studies resulted in prolific and profound writings on doctrines of grace and predestination and the incorporeality of the soul. He thought of evil as the deprivation of good; that before the Fall, humans were free both to sin and not to sin, but in the fallen condition, are free only to sin. It is the grace of Christ that restores the freedom not to sin; within its limits in each of our various stages as human beings, our will is free to determine itself. He taught that we achieve salvation by doing good works aided by divine grace. *City of God,* 426 A.D.

Saint Francis of Assisi. b. Francis Bernadone in Umbria, Italy, c. 1182, d. 1226. An extravagant, profligate youth who was to become the founder of the Franciscan Order of the Catholic Church and the patron saint of environmentalists. After a vision at Spoleto in 1206, he began a life of devotion to the poor and the sick, and to the restoration of churches. He was de-

nounced and disinherited by his father as a madman and retired to a little chapel at Portiuncula where he established rules of simplicity, humility, and poverty for his followers, many of them wealthy and influential men. (It is said he fashioned the first crib at the Hermitage in Grecchio, a custom which endures to this day.) In 1224, he retired to a cell on Mt. Alvena and there received the STIGMATA. During his lifetime, he had numerous supernatural experiences and influenced thousands by his dedication to poverty, his gentleness and compassion, and his delight in animals and in the works of God as revealed in nature. He was canonized in 1228. The first Sunday of October has been designated a time to remember this Christian saint who demonstrated a life of sensitivity to the younger kingdoms.

Saint Hildegard of Bingen. b. 1098, d. 1179. Prolific writer and prophetess, known as the "the Sibyl of the Rhine," was subject to supernatural religious experiences from early childhood. In 1136 she was made Abbess of Rupertsberg and began recording her visions. She was widely influential among kings and prelates, and esteemed for her mysticism, especially by the Holy Roman Emperor, Frederick Barbarossa. Her most noted work is *Scivia,* in which she recorded twenty-six mystical experiences and prophesied great disasters.

Saint Teresa of Avila. b. Castile, Spain, 1515, d. 1582. Carmelite nun and founder of convents for women wishing to lead a more spiritual life than possible under the disregard for rules then prevalent. She established practices of strict enclosure, silence, austerity, coarse clothing and sandals, and perpetual abstinence. The first was called The Monastery of the Discalced (unshod) Carmelites. She gave to Saint John of the Cross, whose *Dark Night of the Soul* recounts his own mystical visions, the task of establishing such refuges for men, while she traveled tirelessly throughout Spain preaching reform despite severe opposition. It was said of her that "few have so united the contemplative and the active life." In 1555 she began to experience visions and hear voices and was tormented by the fear that they were inspired by the devil. After suffering much spiritual desolation, she met St. Peter of Alcantara, who declared her supernatural experiences to be of divine origin. By order of her confessor, she recorded them. She is today considered the discoverer of SEED THOUGHT meditation through her inner spiritual connection, calling her system *"oracion de quietud,"* or prayer of quietude. *Autobiography,* 1565; *Way of Perfection,* 1573; *Interior Castle,* 1577.

Saint Thomas Aquinas. b. Aquino, Italy, 1225, d. 1274. Highly influential theologian and Doctor of the Church who entered the Dominican Order in 1245, devoting his life to the study of the fundamental questions of creation and purpose, mind and matter, will, the soul, human conduct, habits, grace, faith, the unity of the intellect, and the eternity of the world. His writings, pronounced heretical in his time because they reflect the Aristotelian philosophy that matter has always existed and thus all souls, "active intellects," are one, are today considered fundamental to Catholic thinking and are papally approved as such. One day in 1273, during Mass, he is said to have experienced a profound mystical insight. The glory of divine knowledge so overwhelmed him that from that time forward he took no interest in intellectuality. *Summa Theologica,* completed 1272; Biography by G. K. Chesterton: *Saint Thomas Aquinas,* 1956.

Salvation. Enlightenment. Mastery of one's spirit, awakening Godhood. The Self-within illumines life with the light of spirit (MONAD). The saving or reigning of oneself from the power of the nonself. From the Latin word *salvus,* meaning "safe."

Samadhi. A Sanskrit word that means "putting together." Deep and profound meditation or absorption in the spirit. Also, the final stage in yogic practice in which the self becomes one with the object of MEDITATION–releasing separative consciousness, entering a state of super-awareness and profound peace, and merging into the One-with-All.

Sanat Kumara. The planetary Logos, Lord of the World, who in the ancient days came from Venus with a number of KUMARAS to assist humanity to anchor its manas–mindstuff–and continues to dwell in SHAMBALLA. Theosophical Society and Bailey materials support this concept.

Sanskrit. Ancient Indic language of Hinduism and the Vedas; the classical literary language of India and the BRAHMINS–not spoken as a living language but used as a bridge to the wisdom of the past. This is the oldest of the Indo-European group of languages. When studying the Hindu culture, the high-caste characters in dramas speak Sanskrit while the lower caste will speak in a more simplified form, akin to Pali, which is the parent of modern Hindi. The relationship to Sanskrit as the recording, preserving language of the East is similar to Latin as the preserving language of the West.

Satori. Merging into the Oneness through meditation.

Sattva. The highest of the three GUNAS, electric qualities influencing all of life. A positive dynamic resulting in mental brightness and the elevation of consciousness. Also known as action (will).

Scientific servers. A category of WORLD SERVERS who work through synthesized head, throat, and sacral chakras to step down the higher PLAN to humanity.

Seance. A prepared circle or gathering under the direction of one or more sensitives for the purpose of making contact with entities, energies, or influences from the more subtle planes.

Second Person of Trinity. The Christ, reflection of the divine Father and Mother in the lower worlds. Great Lord Christ exists as planetary guide to the source for our planetary stream of life, and the CHRIST-WITHIN, or MYSTICAL CHRIST, is the reflection for individual lives.

Seed atom. A reservoir of data encoded to preserve information to be used in the evolutionary pattern of an individual on a very specific level of expression.

Seed thought. A word, phrase, or sentence used as a focal point in the active form of meditation to unfold consciousness and increase contact with the inner and higher worlds. We meditate upon these "dehydrated thoughts" to reconstitute the greater meaning.

Seed thought meditation. A method of meditation wherein the practitioner takes a posture to penetrate the veil that separates lower mind from higher mind. The seed thought is examined from four viewpoints–form, quality, purpose, and cause–to penetrate beyond the veiled or rational meaning and to perceive the deeper insight available in higher mind.

self. Written with a lower-case *s*, designates the personality.

Self. Written with a capital *S*, denotes the divine Ego or higher Self.

Self-actualization (also self-realization). The process of understanding and fulfilling the self, activating awareness of the high nature to express freely through the personality, allowing for greater self-determination. *See* Maslow, Abraham.

Self-esteem. Recognizing the value of oneself, holding oneself in a position of respect and appreciation.

Self-image. The picture of oneself held in consciousness. This picture may be conscious or unconscious, positive or not, and recognized or not.

Self-mastery. Overcoming the nonself by developing the qualities of the real Self. The first work is to KNOW THYSELF. We proceed to discover the Self and bring its qualities into fullness. The subsequent injunction is to "forget Self" and simply be available to the oneness, moment to moment.

Self-sacrifice. An Agni theme. SACRIFICE means "to make sacred"; so in the practice of self-sacrifice, we purify and bless our life so the self-within can come to life and express its nature. High creativity and becoming the vessel for the soul result as the self is made sacred. Allowing the self to flow through and into the outer form is the work. Correlates to the energy and influence of the number 3.

Sensar. The mysterious language of the MIND that transfers great quantities of knowing into the mind mechanism in a rapid but not linear manner. The knowing then must be transferred to words to be able to articulate the information that has been given.

Sensitives. Those who have a natural or developed ability to perceive with extended or astral senses. Conscious of the reality beyond the physical through the astral, or feeling, nature, such people sense and may be more acutely aware of the thoughts and feelings of others and of occurrences in distant places. Those with an ability to receive impressions and information not generally accessible to others. Sometimes called sensor.

Sephiroth (sephirah, singular). The ten sephiroth of the TREE OF LIFE from the Kabalah are: Kether, crown; Chokmah, wisdom; Binah, intelligence, "Superior Mother"; Chesed, mercy; Geburah, severity and judgment; Tiphareth, beauty; Netzach, victory; Hod, splendor (of the mind); Yesod, foundation; Malkuth, kingdom. *See individual entries.*

Seraphim. Angels of an advanced order who act as the cohesive force in the operation of all life. The word is derived from the Hebrew seraphs, meaning "love"– and these beings represent universal love and fiery enthusiasm. This celestial hierarchy of Gemini is also known as the Lords of Mercury and brings a Ray 3 influence.

Serpent. "Be wise as serpents and pure as doves." (Matthew 10.16) The symbol of wisdom and transformation because it grows, sheds its skin, and transforms time and time again. Used also for the transformational force, called serpentine power or, in Hindu, KUNDALINI, the sleeping energy of evolution awaiting awakening. Due to the healing power of spiritual force and TRANSFORMATION, the serpent became an integral part of the caduceus, the physicians' symbol of two serpents (one black, one white) entwined about a central column and rising to its height. The 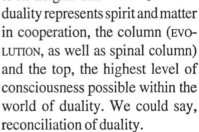 duality represents spirit and matter in cooperation, the column (EVOLUTION, as well as spinal column) and the top, the highest level of consciousness possible within the world of duality. We could say, reconciliation of duality.

Service. Efforts performed for others as an act of generosity from the true self. Acts can vary; we can give from any level of self, but intent and motivation make a major difference determining service from ego play. Service is necessary in that we must "pour out" in order to create a space to receive once again.

Also, an Agni theme. As we pledge ourselves to service, we enter the field of duty and honor. True service is the sharing of our true nature with others; pouring from the self creates an openness into which more can be drawn. Service is the reason for being. Correlates to the energy and influence of the number 9.

Seth materials. Jane Roberts (1929-84), a modern-day amanuensis, received material for several books from an entity, Seth, who taught through her.

"Seven becomes twelve." This is the side of evolution journeying back to the divine manifestation. Seven planes exist as spirit travels Earthward, but on the ascent side, twelve segments exist. Thus we see twelve disciples surround the Christ, twelve months to the solar year, etc. The numbers 1+2 equal three, or the return to the Trinity achieved. *See* One becomes three; Three becomes seven.

Seven Great Officials of the Rays. CHOHANS who distribute the force of each RAY, using many subdepartments and offices. Ray 1, Morya; Ray 2, Kuthumi; Ray 3,

Serapis; Ray 4, The Venetian; Ray 5, Hilarion; Ray 6, Jesus; Ray 7, St. Germaine. *See* MASTERS, THE.

Seven sacred planets. Saturn, Jupiter, Mars, Sun, Venus, Mercury, and Moon are more advanced than Earth on their paths of ascent as they have already awakened to their purpose in the Plan, according to Madame BLAVATSKY.

Shadow. A Jungian term for the incomplete, less refined, and ineptly expressed potential within each of us. CARL JUNG taught that our dreams reveal our shadows–aspects of ourselves we do not realize in our awakened state.

Shadowing. A term used in PSYCHOGRAPHY for attachments and possessions that need to be dissolved or released to a higher level and then replaced with a positive influence, such as the High Self, the Christ, or the Inner Knower.

Shakti. This Sanskrit word, meaning "power, strength, and might," refers to the energy of the supreme, or divine, Mother. The female generative power of energy in the universe; FOHAT is the masculine. Also, the feminine aspect of the spiritual force residing within each human being called KUNDALINI, and one part of the combined forces.

Shalom. The Hebrew word for "peace," and a POWER WORD when spoken as a MANTRA.

Shaman. One who can deliberately shift levels of consciousness and serve as a guide between realities; a practitioner of SHAMANISM.

Shamanism. Practices that associate the self and the world of nature aligned to crystals, plants, and animals. The knowledge and use of such entities for purposes of healing, divination, protection, or gaining greater wisdom.

Shamballa. The sacred island of esoteric tradition referred to as the City of the Gods in ancient mysticism and as Shamballa in more modern writings. Headquarters of the Lord of the World, the primary center through which the will of God is imparted for planetary life. There is debate about whether Shamballa is located in a hidden physical setting, perhaps in the Gobi Desert area, or in the higher ethers of the physical plane.

Shanti. Hindi for "peace," in the sense of *shalom* or *mir*, as in the peace that passes understanding, or the peace of God.

Sheaths of personality. The wrappings of body, emotions, and mind through which the ego functions and with which it often identifies.

Shell. Often a symbol of Baptism since a scallop shell or metal vessel of that shape was used for pouring water over the head of the one being baptized.

Shinto. A religion of Japan and Korea marked by the veneration of ancestors and the powers of nature as points of consciousness–similar to MAYA and Native American beliefs.

Shiva. In HINDUISM, the dissolver or destroyer aspect of God, related to the third person of the Christian trinity.

Shustah. Translates literally "footsteps back to Truth"–in Sanskrit *shus* means "returning footpath," and *tah* means "to truth." A school of spiritual thought and a deck of spiritual symbols for purposes of stimulating the psychic/intuitive senses. Created by ANN MANSER, teacher from St. Petersburg, FL, now deceased.

Siddha Yoga. *See* Yoga.

Siddhis. The diverse phenomena that attest to spiritual compatibility or results from spiritual disciplines, though not spiritual in their own nature. An example would be meditators who demonstrate abilities, i.e., hopping or flying in particular postures.

Silence. A major discipline of spiritual traditions practiced for the purpose of inner discovery. Practices begin with ceasing to talk or responding only when addressed, and progress to maintaining a state of inner and outer quiet. Gradually many layers are peeled away, and we become attuned to the sound current of silence.

Silent watcher. A title given to the solar angel who watches over the development of the immature human soul until it reaches the fourth initiation.

Silver cord. The cord of consciousness – invisible to physical reality – which allows us to leave the physical body, yet remain linked to the physical body while in ASTRAL TRAVEL or projection. Often noted in the OUT-OF-BODY EXPERIENCE (OBE) or NEAR-DEATH EXPERIENCE (NDE) as a silver cord, it looks like an umbilical cord and is attached at the solar plexus, heart, or top of head.

Simplicity. Increased clarity, diminished distortion or illusion, realizing a state wherein absence of complication of understanding results because more integration of Self has occurred.

Sin. A way of learning by following the nonself and the prompting of the senses. From the Greek *amartia*, which translates "to miss the mark." The word in religious teachings for violation of prescribed moral codes. Self-Inflicted Nonsense.

Smudging. A preparation of sweet grass or herbs burned for the purpose of cleaning the astral level of a person or area, usually in preparation for a spiritual service or to attend a spiritual ceremony. Often used to help clear the consciousness of negative influences of heart and mind.

Solar Angel. A member of the HIERARCHY – not of the angelic kingdom–having knowledge of the PLAN and dedicated to the protective care of Earth's evolving human souls. These patient and wise ones volunteered to assist humanity – a threatened and sluggish new kingdom at an early time of crisis. The Solar Angel on its own path of solar initiation gains merit for its work with humanity. Its principal duties are to act as a transformer for the powerful streams of energy from the Soul to the personality and to vibrate the Plan for humanity at the edge of the conscious mind. A Solar Angel for an individual soul is the SILENT WATCHER until the individual matures (the fourth INITIA-TION in esoteric Christian tradition).

Solar deities. Heavenly beings embodied in a solar system and advancing through the expanded consciousness of each planet within the system. Our heavenly being contains all of our planets—which are centers of awareness, the Sun being the heart.

Solar initiation. Differentiates between the lunar-astral development which guided humanity during involution and the development of the conscious mind on the evolutionary path of ascent. Also, the advanced initiations of the Soul which follow the human initiations when the mature Soul continues its experience in service through yet another evolving set of experiences to better reflect the MONAD. The monad completes the cycle as it satisfies the cosmic initiation requirements.

Solar Logos. A cosmic entity who affects all lesser lives in evolution within our solar system through application of will and intelligence. The Sun is the physical vehicle of the Great Life called the Solar Logos through which divine will is radiated toward each planet. This RING-PASS-NOT comprises the entire circumference of the solar

system—and everything included within the sphere of influence of the Sun. The Solar Logos is the sum total of all manifestation within that sphere—from the lowest and densest physical atom to the most radiant and cosmic, ethereal DHYANI CHOHAN. Contained within it are seven planetary logoi, whose physical bodies are the PLANETS of our solar system and who act as the centers through which the Solar Logos pours forth its force and purpose.

Solar mysteries. The mysteries to which the conscious mind must awaken on the path of evolution. Also, the three primary mysteries of the solar system: 1) the mystery of electricity, 2) the mystery of polarity, and 3) the mystery of fire itself—the secrets of the third, second, and first aspects of divine life, respectively.

Solar Yoga. See Yoga.

Solemnity. An Agni term. Respectful thought, honor, and nobility of intent; appropriate regard for concepts to be held high, revered, and exalted. The ability to see why each concept is holy and to respond in kind. *See* Reverence.

Solstice. When the Sun is the most distant from the equator—southernmost or northernmost—the longest and the shortest days of the year occur in the respective hemispheres. Summer solstice is celebrated in the northern hemisphere as the Sun moves from Gemini to Cancer, at the height of the growing and flowering season. At winter solstice, when the light is hidden, we go within and renew our commitment as the Sun moves from Sagittarius to Capricorn.

Sons of God. A way of speaking of sparks of God that descend to embody and learn through experience within matter.

Sophia. One of the names for God used frequently in the Jewish scriptures and the Greek word for "wisdom" in the original Greek of the Bible. Here is the divine validation of the holy feminine spirit, co-eternal, co-creator with God. "I, Sophia, was there when the heavens were prepared." (Proverbs 8.27) Numerous sages of Western spirituality–Hermes Trismegistus, Solomon, Pythagoras, Heraclitus, St. Thomas Aquinas, Hildegard of Bingen, Carl Jung–have acknowledged Wisdom as the divine feminine spirit of ANDROGYNY, immortality, and wholeness. Sophia is often seen as a female emanation or persona of the true God distorted in the world of appearances. Many gnostic systems depict her as WISDOM that becomes distorted in the false world of creation.

Sophia of Jesus Christ. An overwriting of the *Eugnostos the Blessed* found as a part of the Nag Hammadi Library. A gnostic text believed from the first century and said to be a teaching given by Master Jesus after his resurrection–"not in his previous form, but in the invisible spirit." This mystic document describes the HIERARCHY of the world of creation and the fall of man into the more dense world. The Savior is sent for the purpose of redemption. In the *Sophia of Jesus Christ,* the Savior is Jesus; in *Eugnostos the Blessed,* the name is not given.

Sorcery. The selfish use of transformational knowledge, often called BLACK MAGIC, for personal gain, money, or fame. The abuse is the use of spiritual powers for the benefit of ego or to the disadvantage of another.

Soul. The expanding spark of divinity within life. The human being's contact with the universal Source, linking personality to MONAD and reflecting monadic presence to developing personality. State of awareness achieved through assistance of SOLAR ANGEL. As awareness increases, the mature human soul becomes less reflection and more the monad itself–a fragment of the OVERSOUL, a spark of the One Flame imprisoned within form. The life aspect which gives the vital factor to each being, life, or consciousness. Some use "Soul" to designate one who, having enhanced and deepened control of the soul over lower aspects, has achieved first initiation–birth of the Christ-within. Others reserve the right to capitalize Soul for the fourth initiation when it is said that we live as a Soul or ADEPT. The soul, considered feminine in nature, is that part of the human that births the inner Christ.

The soul of man is like to water;
From heaven it cometh,
To heaven it riseth
And then returneth to earth,
For ever alternating...
Goethe
Song of the Spirits Over the Waters

Soul alignment. The goal of all MEDITATION. Specific techniques have evolved as the receiver set is built and expanded to be responsive to increasingly subtle influences. Alignment leads to response to impressions, RAY influence, higher will, and greater love. Thus we take our places in alignment to our individual and GROUP SOUL purposes.

Soul astrology. An understanding held in ESOTERIC ASTROLOGY of a method to determine the purpose the soul seeks to realize in a particular incarnation.

Soul attunement. The harmonizing vibration of two or more souls for the purpose of assisting one another. A name for a reading regarding the purpose of the soul and/or facilitating the goal of establishing personality in right-alignment to soul.

Soul growth. A more conscious use of soul power and more complete expression of soul qualities at a personality level. The development of the physical, emotional, and mental bodies – or "personality"– into a mechanism through which the human soul anchored in the spiritual triad can express itself in the three lower worlds and use them as a field of service.

Soul infusion. The state in which a coworking relationship between the soul and the personality has been achieved. When the real personality – the totality of the three LOWER BODIES – has been developed and integrated with the soul. The process of soul infusion–in which the light of the unit created by Soul and SOLAR ANGEL illumines the personality–stimulates a greater radiation of the divine within matter. This stage is also known as the mystic marriage and is associated with the third initiation of the esoteric Christian tradition, TRANS-FIGURATION.

Soul purpose. The goal of an incarnation; the experience the soul desired that prompted it to create and experience through a personality.

Soulmate. One or more souls of such a close vibrational frequency to assist each other in realizing the desired growth pursued by either and both during incarnation.

Soulstar. The symbol of a bright star over the head is used to represent the presence of the soul (and SOLAR ANGEL) from which the personality has descended, and continues to be overlighted, an archetype to constantly remind personality of its source of power and true nature. Imaged over a person's head during exercises when invoking soul influence. This soul energy is significant to the process of emanation and TRANSFORMATION.

Sound current. The generative first word–the sacred sound, the OM–that went forth and continues to reverberate. This silent, mystic tone that underlies creation, "the Word" or "divine sound," can be heard with the inner ear as it continues to create and maintain the universe.

Space. The seemingly empty, receptive void; more commonly, the openness in which the planets revolve. However, there is no true emptiness, for all Creation is manifestation, but a less dense cup is necessary for a space to invite or be receptive to purpose. Less dense space allowed manifestation to enter into its womb for the purpose of spirit. Thus space, the void, is the divine feminine, the receiver and participator with spirit in the act of creation.

Spacial beings. A parallel kingdom to humanity evolving in dimensions of the Earth humanity doesn't frequently explore. Extended by definition to other evolving intelligences transferred to Earth from other planets in the greater space of the Universe. Also called extra-terrestrials, ETs, space brothers.

Spacial kingdom. This kingdom has its center on the mental plane, and its beings are able to project into denser dimensions.

Spark, divine. The MONAD; a particle of the creative FOHAT which travels into the dense realities in

INVOLUTION and returns to the Source through the process of EVOLUTION.

Sparks of spacial consciousness. This Agni term is used with "superradiant fires of space" to describe fohat imaged as a form of primal energy-matter with a greater emphasis on energy pouring forth to permeate all of creation: the innate consciousness that we might call "spark of God."

Specific works (of meditation). Meditation can be employed for a wide variety of needs, purposes, and experiential works: healing, directing energy to others, opening the heart center, sustaining another, telepathy. The purpose determines the technique used.

Spirit. A term derived from the Latin word *spiritus* for "breath." The divine spark within each soul, the breath, or spirit, of God, i.e., Holy Spirit. Also, widely used as meaning all nonmaterial beings.

Spirit attachment. A point of consciousness which becomes attracted to another and takes up a parasitic relationship using or affecting the energy of another. The host may or may not be aware of this attachment. EXORCISM or SPIRIT RELEASEMENT is needed to free both the host and parasite.

Spirit guides. One or a number of friends in spirit who collect around a human to provide encouragement and assistance.

Spirit releasement therapy. Techniques developed to release attachments and free the host; a modern term for "exorcism."

Spiritual. Having to do with the evolving soul. Distinguished from "religious" dogmas and teachings by following the promptings and personal teachings of the spirit within self.

Spiritual disciplines. Practices embraced to enhance an awareness of the spirit within. Most religious, as well as spiritual, traditions encourage some spiritual disciplines–sometimes specific exercises and rules of conduct, such as diet (vegetarianism), prayer, meditation, silence, poverty (owning no property), celibacy, service to others. These "practices of disciples" may be either or both additions and/or subtractions to daily life.

Spiritual healing. The art and science of working with the subtle energies for the purpose of improving or harmonizing the level of self to facilitate health or healing.

Spiritual law. Reference to the HERMETIC PRINCIPLES as we know them. Seven great laws that guide all life in its evolving consciousness and express through numerous lesser laws, ever just, ever imprinting the law of justice into humanity. Collective influences that maintain and support life through its processes of creation, orderliness, and destruction. The basic laws are generally enumerated as seven and most commonly called the Hermetic Principles. Within the framework of this structure, numerous operations of cause and effect have been defined. The seven great laws are the Principles of 1) Mentalism, 2) Correspondence, 3) Vibration, 4) Polarity, 5) Rhythm, 6) Cause and Effect, 7) Gender.

Spiritual messengers. Those who descend to the outer world bringing a specific "word," message, or work to be delivered to outer reality. Some associate this term with "WALK-IN," as coined by author Ruth Montgomery.

Spiritual politics. A new grasp of the work of Ray 1 is emerging as the true nature of politics is becoming known. The concept is that everything begins in mysticism and ends in politics. As we comprehend with spiritual insight, we realize that spiritual politics explores the effects from the inside to the outer, not from the outer toward the inner. Spiritual politics seeks to explain the interconnectedness of all events.

Spiritual science. The evolution of high consciousness as it relates to the human being, to the Universe, and all creation, as taught by the ageless wisdom, occult studies, and theosophy.

Spiritual teacher. One more wise–little or great–who shares with others what s/he has *realized* in order to give comfort and assurance as to goals, to mark the route of spiritual conquest for others.

Spiritual Triad. The reflection of the divine trinity within the human being: ATMA-BUDDHI-MANAS, or spiritual will, intuition, and higher mind. Also called the "Spiritual Human"–the levels of which are built with atmic, buddhic, and manasic substance, or light substance. The expression of the MONAD, the germinal seed containing divine potential that unfolds during the course of evolution. This expression creates the soul which in turn creates the personality.

Spiritual will. The will of soul or spirit within self with which we seek to blend personality will, that the higher may be expressed.

Spiritualism. An aspect of the Christian religion that focuses on issues concerning life after death; interaction between the so-called dead and those inhabiting physical bodies, and on-going life in the more subtle realities. Communication between the planes is a major emphasis.

Spirituality. The expression of the essence of oneself. As activity is focused on the innermost dimension of an individual, the essence – called Self, soul and/or spirit by most esoteric traditions – opens and shares its transcendental nature of reality. Spiritual paractices are to explore this core and to facilitate a greater expression of the spiritual sacred within called "consciousness" or "soul maturity."

Spontaneity. Freedom to release barriers and limitations that restrict the full flow of the animated spirit and its consciousness within life.

Sri Rama. An AVATAR well known in the Hindu tradition. One of the principal avatars of Vishnu; next to Krishna, the most popular deity of Vishnuism.

Star people. Those believed to have incarnated in the human family, having transferred to planet Earth from elsewhere in the universe.

Stations of the Cross. Fourteen depictions of the life of Jesus, the Christ, depicting the mysteries of the PATH OF INITIATION. The first seven focus on the WATER MYSTERIES, the last seven on the FIRE MYSTERIES. Often a practice during Lent when we become mindful of initiations and truly express love for the wayshower and the service he rendered to the Christ and humanity. Rarely understood for its esoteric meaning and a practice that may easily degenerate into a mere recognition of the life and suffering of Jesus.

Steiner, Rudolf. b. Austria, 1861, d. 1925. Mystic, clairvoyant, and founder of the Anthroposophical Society, which drew on Rosicrucian, theosophical, and Christian traditions that expressed belief in a spiritual world available to those possessing the highest faculties of intellect, though accessible through training to all. He believed that the mind had to be made to rise above its material preoccupations to gain realization of spiritual reality. Steiner's lectures led to a widespread interest in biodynamic farming and the use of natural fertilizers. The Waldorf Schools with instruction based on color, form, rhythm, and nature studies are still actively attended today. EURYTHMY, the art of move-

177

ment to speech and sound as conceived by Steiner, has led to the music therapies and healing-with-sound techniques in current use. *Cosmic Memory Prehistory: of Earth and Man,* 1968; *Man as Symphony of the Creative World,* 1970; *Art in the Light of Mystery Wisdom,* 1970; *The Inner Nature of Music and the Experience of Tone,* 1983.

Stigmata. From the Greek word meaning "brand." Spontaneous marks, wounds, or bleeding – corresponding to the wounds Jesus, the Christ, suffered on the cross – that appear on the physical bodies of mystics. *See* Saint Francis of Assisi.

Straight gate. Esoterically, Path of Initiation.

Straight knowledge. Revelation; intuitive knowledge received directly from the higher realities.

Striving. An Agni theme. Keeping ourselves in a state of creative tension and using passion to propel the self toward high consciousness is "striving." As we strive, the astral body becomes purified and provides strength with which to live a refined life. Correlates to the energy of the number 1.

Subconscious, the. The storehouse of knowledge held individually or collectively to be utilized by various levels of mind, consciously or not.

Sub-Ray (or sub-plane). The influence of a Ray expressing on a lower cycle (or sub-plane) within the greater cycle of another Ray influence.

Subtle body. Generally the etheric form, the nonphysical, etheric vehicle which looks like the physical manifestation and can separate from the physical body and travel alone through the etheric/astral reality.

Sufism. A Moslem ascetic, mystic sect, originally associated with Islamic tradition (8th century, Persian). Now often meant as a mysticism free from association with formal tradition.

Sun behind the Sun. The real Sun hidden behind the visible Sun which is only its reflection or its shell. The Sun is the storehouse of all the energy of our universe–the heart of the solar system; the ever-hidden, attracting, and emitting life center. Also known as the Central Spiritual Sun and regarded as the primal source of Being; the center of Universal Life-Electricity; the reservoir in which divine radiance is focused. According to esoteric teaching, behind the visible Sun is the Great Heart – the source of the outpouring love of the Creator. Hidden behind that invisible Sun is the Central Spiritual Sun which is the source of all life. Acknowledged by astronomical science as the presence in space of a central body in the Milky Way – a point unseen and mysterious. The physical Sun is regarded as the physical expression of the Central Spiritual Sun which is hidden by the great brilliance of the visible manifestation. In esoteric literature: the True Sun "who givest sustenance to the Universe, from whom all proceed and to whom all return." The universe is believed to have evolved from this Central Sun, or point, which is the ever-concealed germ of all life. Therefore, it is the source not only of our physical Sun but of all the Suns and of all universes; the Super-Solar Being that pulsates its creative will pursuant to the rhythm of the divine Plan. *See* Yoga, Solar.

Sun of Righteousness. An ancient title given to the Sun, the heart of the solar system, and the reflection of the COSMIC CHRIST which loves, energizes, and sustains our universe.

Sun sign. The constellation in which the Sun is located at the time of birth. Considered to be the principal point of one's personal chart, the Sun sign represents our inner developing self–the personality or ego. The Moon (sign) and the ascendant are the other two most significant points of the personal trinity. Twelve in number, dividing the year into periods exhibiting similar qualities and attributes. An EPHEMERIS is used to establish exactness of the position of planets at any given time.

Superconscious. The part of the God-self where we connect to the whole.

Survival of the fittest, law of. That which can best cope adapts in order to continue; all else is swept away.

Sushumna. One of the channels in the subtle body through which the KUNDALINI power ascends when awakened along the spinal column. This central canal in the finer body is located and traversed by means of spiritual practice according to the careful instructions of a teacher. The current on the left is called IDA, and that on the right is known as PINGALA.

Sutratma. This one of three threads forming the ANTAHKARANA is anchored in the heart. When it is withdrawn, the physical body dies. Also known as the "life thread."

Svadharma. The truth of one's own path, the inner path of spiritual truth, addressed in the *Bhagavad Gita* (18.47): "Better to follow one's own svadharma (inner law), however humble, than to follow another's, though great. By engaging in the work prescribed by one's own soul, one does not miss the mark."

Swami. A title given to one spiritually prepared to serve, much like a Hindu priest. Traditionally swamis are trained in an apprentice style, working closely with their guru and very aware of their lineage. *See* Paramahansa Yogananda.

Symbology. The study of pictures, images, designs, and glyphs as a way of awakening vast amounts of archetypal knowledge in a simple manner. This international, cross-cultural language of MYTHS, DREAMS, VISIONS, and RITUAL is timeless and limitless compared to words – a wonderful tool for the SUB- and SUPERCONSCIOUS!

Synchronicity. A Jungian term: the coincidences of life that reveal the greater, unitive pattern existing outside our normal awareness or perception. What appears as separate actions developing and moving toward a single point of connection, often considered divine timing, sometimes recognized, sometimes not.

Synthesis. The increasing ability to see the dovetailing of diverse actions and manifestations of life to create an evolution of awareness. These energies blend into a newness that integrates what appear to be unrelated actions.

An Agni term to describe a moment of coming together, a time of achievement brought about by a unique blending of energies. It is the work of Rays 1 and 7 to synthesize forces present and to create anew.

T

Ta'i Chi. A system of graceful and gentle postures, almost dancelike, that facilitates the movement of life force *(chi)* throughout the body. Health- and strength-giving, the practice is often referred to as a "moving meditation."

Tamas. The lowest of the three gunas, the influence of electric qualities affecting all of life. This negative influence of sluggishness is also described as stability (inertia).

Tantric Yoga. *See* Yoga.

Taoism. An Eastern world religion following the teachings of Lao-Tzu. The Tao (pronounced with a *d* rather than *t* sound), or the "Way," emphasizes passivity and living gently: "By non-action everything can be done." "Be humble and you will remain entire; be bent and you will remain straight." And "He who knows does not speak; he who speaks does not know."

Tao Te Ching. Lao-Tzu's "Book of the Way" is the Taoist classic manual on the art of living, in eighty-one brief chapters.

Tapes. Memories of impressions and experiences of the earlier years of this life and previous lives held at a less-than-conscious level of mind. Often referred to as "programming." "Old tapes"– a reference to the reenactment of past experience by the mind – impede spiritual advancement.

Tara. An Eastern term popular to Buddhism, meaning "fountain" and referring to a female Master. A representation of the divine feminine; divine Shakti. Known to the Tibetans as Dolma, the Saviouress, the Great Goddess of Mercy (or in Sanskrit, *Tara),* and revered by

Mongols and Tibetans as a female emanation of AVALOKITA, a great Master.

Teacher of Righteousness. A title given in the updated teachings of the Essene tradition for the holy one who would provide guidance from God. Some suspect the ESSENES saw Master Jesus as destined to serve in this capacity.

Teilhard de Chardin, Pierre. b. Sarcenat, France, 1881, d. 1955. Jesuit priest, theologian, and paleontologist (he participated in the discovery of Peking man while on expedition in China), noted for his interpretation of Christianity in the perspective of cosmic evolution, which became central to his scientific and religious thought. He envisioned a new advancement of humanity toward the Omega Point – Christogenesis, the goal of the evolutionary process. At this point, all things reach a suprapersonal unity in God, in which agapé, or self-transcending, love prevails. *Phenomenon of Man,* 1959; *The Divine Milieu,* 1960.

Telepathic communicators. Those with the ability to communicate thoughts from mind to mind. Also, a category of WORLD SERVERS who work through integrated head, heart, and throat to step down the higher plan for humanity.

Temple. A dwelling place for the holy. A place within ourselves, such as a dedicated heart, or in the outer world that has been purified and dedicated to spiritual purposes.

Tension. An Agni term. The pull of consciousness toward evolution that results in psychological stretch first and spiritual transformation in time. This evolutionary tug creates a degree of tension underlying all creation.

Tesla, Nikola. b. Croatia, 1856, d. 1943. Physicist and electrical engineer who worked at Menlo Park. After quarreling with Thomas Edison, he left to devote himself to his own inventions: improved dynamos, transformers, electric bulbs, and the Tesla high-frequency coil. Today many feel they are being inspired by Tesla from spirit to investigate alternative sources of energy to help humanity with current ecological challenges.

Theosophical Society. An association established in 1875 by Helena Blavatsky, Charles Leadbeater, Annie Besant, and Charles Olcott. It still thrives worldwide today, with a large audience. Its American headquarters are in Wheaton, Illinois. *See individual biographies.*

Theosophy. The philosophy of the revealed teachings given by Madame Helena P. Blavatsky covering the nature, structure, origin, destiny, and operations of the universe – and meaning "divine wisdom." Mme. Blavatsky was inspired greatly by ancient Tibetan and Hindu beliefs.

"There are no accidents." Acknowledging "Higher will, not mine," and revealing underlying perception that the Higher has a reason for all actions. Nothing happens without a cause. There are no accidents, only ways and means of calling us to a higher awareness.

Third eye. The instrument of true spiritual vision and insight to be developed at the center of the forehead in etheric matter. The etheric correspondence of the pineal gland which sees, creates, communicates, heals, destroys obstacles, unveils mysteries, and controls and directs energies. This faculty allows us to see the blueprint of creative imagination on the mental level and to visualize creatively on that plane. Commonly confused with the astral forehead center associated with clairvoyance and mistakenly called the third eye. An etheric center of energy and force that is an instrument of will or spirit. The eye of inner vision through which we can direct and control the energy of matter, see all things in the eternal now, and be aware of causes more than effects. This esoteric organ is the medium through which direct and certain knowledge is obtained; it does not convey clairvoyance. Also referred to as the single or spiritual eye, Eye of Shiva, EYE OF HORUS, and the ruby eye of the serpent. *See* Alder, Vera Stanley.

Third initiation. Midpoint of the human path of INITIATION when both heart and mind are integrated, well developed, and purified sufficiently to be subjected to the will of the soul. Also known as SOUL INFUSION.

Thoughtform. The etheric picture, pattern, or form created on the mental plane by the active mind –somewhat like an etching – that dissolves easily unless energized by the emotional nature. Real thought is the life-principle of any thoughtform. When this real thought or vital principle is withdrawn, the thoughtform exists for a while as a corpse in the mental sea until it disintegrates. All physical forms originally were thoughtforms in someone's mind that have taken shape.

"Three becomes seven." As it leaves the realm of the MONAD (or the 1), the TRINITY (or the 3) is ani-

Three-brain concept. The animal part of our being operates from the REPTILIAN BRAIN (1), i.e., the sympathetic nervous system that keeps us autonomically breathing, digesting, and performing other involuntary functions. Its greatest concern is survival. The MAMMALIAN (2), or mid-brain, knows the need for socialization; this is the seat of self-esteem. The NEOCORTEX (3) is the center of ego structure as a result of human INDIVIDUATION and is divided into left and right hemispheres, each with its own characteristics:

Left hemisphere:
- masculine in nature
- rational
- cognitive
- analytical
- positive
- sequential
- linear
- active
- goal-oriented
- concrete
- explicit

Right hemisphere:
feminine in nature
artistic • intuitive • playful
imaginative • physical
gentle • spontaneous
diffuse • visual
holistic • emotional
nonverbal

mated at the ATMIC level with seven types of will, or RAYS. The 3 now becomes 7 in expression. *See* "One becomes three," and "Seven becomes twelve."

Three worlds of mind. The worlds, or planes, ruled by the Great Mind, usually identified as physical (brain), astral (desire mind), and the mental mechanism (instinctual mind). Behind these three resides divine mind which is the creator impulse. *See* Mind; Mental planes; Instinctual mind.

Thrones. The hierarchical rulership of the Lords of Karma, the LIPIKAS, expressing through the constellation of Taurus. These angels represent the force of God through which divine law and judgments are generated. The Thrones represent the function of rulership and are associated with Ray 1–the Universal Will as expressed in evolution, or God the Father. They contemplate the glory and equity of supreme judgments, teach humanity to rule with justice, and act as the bridge between destiny and karma.

Tibetan, the. *See* Djwhal Khul.

 Tiphareth. The sixth sephirah on the kabalistic TREE OF LIFE equates to Beauty and is the principal sephirah of the tree, for here the sun/son is represented and the upper and lower faces overlap. The home of divine consciousness.

Tongues, speaking in. The Pentecostal experience of speaking and hearing in a variety of languages with those in spiritual grace who are capable of understanding and being understood. Known as one of the GIFTS OF SPIRIT (1 Corinthians 12). A practice of some Christian denominations to demonstrate spiritual status. In Esoteric Christianity it is understood as an experience that occurs when a great deal of emotion/devotion moves through the emotional nature, manifesting in an altered state of consciousness and a stimulation of the throat chakra. The words spoken may or may not be understood by the speaker, but biblical teaching is that one will always be present who can understand "the soul crying out to its God."

Toning. A technique using sound to move energy through the personality to release blocks and balance the centers. Rediscovered by Laurel Elizabeth Keyes who developed and taught a psychological approach–toning–to many. Her book, *Toning–the Creative Power of the Voice,* is available through DeVorss and Company.

Root chakra –
    sound O, as in Om
2nd chakra –
    sound U, as in oo
Solar plexus chakra –
    sound A, as in ah
Heart chakra – sound E, as in ay
Throat chakra – sound I, as in ee
Brow chakra –
    sound MMM or NNN
Crown chakra –
    sound NNG, or silence

Trained observers. A particular category of WORLD SERVERS who work through integrated head, heart, and solar plexus to step down the higher plan for humanity.

Trance. A reference to an altered state of consciousness. States may vary from a light and slight brain wave frequency change to a significant alteration wherein the entranced person cannot remember or recall the event, words said, or what happened while undergoing the experience. Entering a trance can be accomplished while alone or with the assistance of another, and for a variety of reasons.

Transcendental. Surpassing the senses; mystical. *See* Transcendental Meditation.

Transcendental field. The mystical awareness beyond rational knowing with which we can interact and an individual can encompass.

Transcendental Meditation (TM). The registered name for a siddha yoga approach to meditation brought to the United States by Maharishi Mahesh Yogi in the late 1960s. A simplified approach with a MANTRA is given to initiates along with techniques and instructions for their use. This approach, emphasizing human potential and scientific evaluation, has resisted the religious connotations of Hinduism to a great degree. It does, however, utilize Eastern culture and mystique.

Transfiguration. The process of creating a new vehicle of expression through the use of fire (purification) and light (of the soul), particularly by the practice of focused meditation. The new vehicle, once evoked, is to serve more perfectly the purposes of soul and spirit. Transfiguration occurs as the electric fire of the spiritual triad pours into the mind of personality, thereby releasing the light of the atoms within the three lower bodies of personality to produce enlightenment. The recreated new vehicle is often called the "mystical wedding garment," the "robe of glory," or the "coat of many colors," as it is created of higher frequencies so that it may reflect more perfectly the energies of the soul and, in time, the Spirit. It is this vehicle that can be uplifted into other planes and come and go without decay.

Transformation. A personality change aligning to a pattern appropriate to spiritual life which so sensitizes the recipient that incoming spiritual forces have significant increased impact. Modern churches try to influence this receptivity to change. Transformation requires the use of will and practices to clear and cleanse the astral and mental vehicles. As the purified astral reflects and the focused mind expands, their refined frequencies capture and reflect higher awareness. In transformation, devotion clears the astral vehicle, and love fills the life with aspiration; as illusions clear, the mind more faithfully reflects high consciousness. These changes emerge as a series of reforms in daily life, initiated by the aspirant.

As an Agni virtue for Scorpio, the processes of magic, alchemy, and change of personality are aspects of transformation. Beginning with self-discipline, we invoke will and choose a path of light, using both the forces of heart (aspiration) and mind (inspiration) to transform both consciousness and lifestyle.

Transmigration. A belief that human souls can incarnate into the bodies of animals–taught by Plato in his earlier works though he appears to abandon the belief in later writings. The UPANISHADS similarly suggest the possibility of animal incarnation.

Transmutation. The continuing process of changes in the very substance of the VEHICLE of personality that begins with the second initiation. The clearing and cleansing effect an actual transmutation from matter to light. The etheric body, now much more reflective of heart and mind, continues to become a more delicate receiver set for high frequencies. Both matter and consciousness vibrate increasingly to the soul. As the etheric body is so sensitized, it has more impact on the body, the aura increases in glow and vibrancy, and more energy flows to the physical body. During transmutation, the astral body, as a separate vehicle, disintegrates, and the energy released moves to create the MYSTICAL MARRIAGE of heart and mind.

Transpersonal. Transcending, or reaching beyond, the individual nature.

Transpersonal self. The inner presence, the Self, the Christ-within, the ATMAN.

Tree of Life. A mythological symbol prevalent in many indigenous world religions, as in Genesis of the Bible. Other mystical approaches use the tree upon which to hang symbols or glyphs representing a variety of energies. The well known kabalistic glyph has become known as the "Tree of Life." However, the Druids, the Maya, and others had their sacred tree as well, sometimes in the center of the known world, at other times with its roots in heaven and its branches in the world of manifestation.

Tree of Life, Kabalah. The glyph upon which ten sephiroth are placed, each of a different energy, or quality. In the descent, the worlds are formed; the person on the path ascends the tree or returns to the higher realities after mastering the lower. Each sephirah has its own name, quality, and color.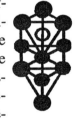

Trefoil. St. Patrick used nature's example of the shamrock in the trefoil–with its three equal lobes–to explain the doctrine of the Trinity.

Triangle. The perfect archetypical and earliest known symbol of the holy TRINITY. The three sides, being equal in length, represent the equality of the three aspects of Divinity.

Tribulation. A period of severe affliction or acute trial for an individual or a group. Many believe we are currently undergoing such a time, as predicted by the Bible.

Trinity. Christian tradition recognizes the concept of deity as three-in-one: Father (-Mother), Son, and Holy Spirit; other world religions do as well. Hinduism: Brahma, Vishnu, Shiva; and Druidism: Beli, the Creator, Taran, controller of the present, and Yesu, the coming savior.

Triquetra. A design of three equal arcs, representing the holy Trinity. Its continuous form symbolizes eternity, and the intertwining represents the indivisibility of the holy Trinity. Used frequently today to represent the interlocking relationship of body, mind, and spirit.

"Turn the other cheek." (Matthew 5.39) An admonishment not to respond to misuse or abuse with vindictiveness but to respond meekly rather than add a negative energy that will prolong the battle. We could say, do not set new karma into action. Attempt to finish the pattern by setting good into motion.

U

Unconscious darkness. A state of evolution whereby we are guided by involution, or instinctual nature; KALI YUGA is the period of purification at this level of planetary life.

Unconscious, the. A level of self of which most are unaware but which contains much instinctual awareness (knowledge that has slipped beneath the level of consciousness) and unawakened potential. Each person has an individual unconscious but also taps into the unconscious of the human race. Also, those who are not yet awakened–considered asleep to higher worlds.

Unforgivingness. This barrier to spiritual growth–the nonreleasing of either self or another–causes us to stay bound in ourselves. Without granting freedom, we cannot make progress to become all we might be.

Unity. The ability to increasingly see beyond separateness, finding the principles that unite perspectives in order to heal and affirm the oneness of life.

Universal law. A way of designating the sustaining axioms of spiritual reality as we can understand them within the human experience. These laws are determined within the framework of the HERMETIC PRINCIPLES. *See* Spiritual law.

Universal Mind (or Consciousness). The mind of God; the consciousness of the Supreme Being which permeates the entire universe. A state of God-consciousness in which the great will or purpose of the Logos is known. Union with God; a state in which the Soul consciously knows itself to be one with the ALL. The vast consciousness with which we are identified–the totality of consciousness. The divine thinker, or principle of intelligence which makes itself known as the will-to-be, desire, or love-of-being, and that active, intelligent purpose which animates the solar system.

Universality. The thread of sameness that flows through all of life. A particular perspective now being discovered as running through many aspects and experiences of life.

The Agni virtue for Gemini. Nonseparativeness. Both a blessing and a challenge, for ultimately universality–the wholeness–is the guiding consciousness of all life. The awareness that no separation or abrupt break exists between life forces because each flows into the other, overlapping and embracing. People of high consciousness stand for one spirit, one life, and one existence to express these interlocking bonds of life.

Universe. A spiritual system governed by the laws of higher reality which reflects divine law at work from the smaller particles to the rhythm of the planets themselves.

Unself, the. Another name for ego, the nonself.

Upanishads. Spiritual writings of the East; a part of the Vedas from which emerged a system of philosophy and spiritual teachings called the Vedanta. The esoteric wisdom of Hinduism is held largely in the Upanishads.

V

Vedanta. A Hindu philosophy derived from the teachings of the UPANISHADS that all reality is a single principle, BRAHMA. The believer's goal is to transcend the limitations of self-identity and realize unity with Brahma.

Vedas. The most ancient sacred literature of the Hindus, consisting of four collections called 1) Rig Veda, hymns to the gods, 2) Sama Veda, priests' chants, 3) Yajur Veda, sacrificial formulae in prose, and 4) Atharva Veda, magical chants. Considered to be "revealed literature," they contain philosophical insights and are regarded as the final authority.

Vehicle. In esoteric terminology, "body." The vehicle of mind expresses thought; the astral (emotional) vehicle expresses feeling; the physical vehicle expresses action.

Veil. A protective covering used to conceal the perception mechanism of the expanding mind. Veils dissolve as consciousness heightens and perception clears.

Veils, four. The veils that separate three inner-plane segments known as the HALLS OF LEARNING are defined by MASTER DJWHAL KHUL. These curtains over the windows of vision prevent the realization of that which is beyond our capability; they block the light of consciousness. They protect the human kingdom from the burning energies we may not yet be able to contact. As we experience INITIATION, we are attuned to handle the fiery currents and can safely rend the veil and advance.

The 1st, the Veil of Impulsion, obscures the Hall of Concentration. This is the veil the average person meets. It is made up of the four OBSTACLES ON THE

PATH. The energy of the veil is Law. To go beyond it, we must realize the purpose of spiritual law and respect it.

The 2nd, the Veil of Distortion, prevents entrance to the Hall of Choice. This veil distorts our picture of reality beyond the physical dimension. The Christ rent this veil by his power of love, symbolizing that those who can love (without glamours) can advance to the fourth initiation. When this occurs, the DWELLER is released and the soul meets itself on the BUDDHIC PLANE. The energy of this veil is love, and we must know love as a great and powerful force to go further.

The 3rd. As the Veil of Separation (between the Hall of Choice and the Hall of Blinded Men) is rent, a brilliant charge of light is released, revealing the union of all. The energy of this veil is union, or synthesis, and it enables progress.

The 4th, the Veil of Aspiration, will be rent by humanity itself when it stands as "massed intent" as the EXTERNALIZATION OF THE HIERARCHY occurs. The energy of the veil is called life, and it will pour forth in a renewed way when the Hierarchy takes physical residence upon the planet once again.

The veils of the temple are representative of the separation formed by outer participation and the inner mystery hidden even from ourselves. *See* Halls of Learning.

Vessel. Symbolically, the receptive consciousness formed through spiritual exercises necessary for spiritual advancement.

Vibration (Hermetic principle of). All is vibrating, in movement – some slower, to be known as matter; some faster, so as to be invisible.

Virtues. Working under the archangels and with the concrete mental and abstract astral substances, this advanced order of angels bestows miracles, evokes integrity, and releases the flow of grace upon humanity. A soul quality clearly expressed as a soul energy is drawn into the personality and flows without distortion through the consciousness of an individual into the physical world. This ability to bring a soul quality into the personality is called "building a virtue or facet of the soul." *See* Astrology.

Vishnu. The second person of the Hindu trinity, the son. Lord KRISHNA is considered an incarnation of Vishnu.

Vision. An experience of higher reality, usually while in an altered state that inspires or conveys direction, response, or action.

Vision of the Aquarian era. Humanity will become aware of unseen life in a way not recognized until spiritual senses evolve to be used. Then as it reaches new heights of vibration the DEVAS will teach humanity: how to nourish the physical body from the ethers, telepathy, and a new use of color and sound. The new MYSTERY SCHOOLS will emerge as the EXTERNALIZATION OF THE HIERARCHY occurs. This is but a glimpse of the vision for which the Aquarian era is to strive!

Vivekananda, Swami. b. India, 1863, d. 1902. Indian yogi and chief disciple of the Christlike Ramakrishna Paramahansa who brought Vedanta to the West. The Vedanta, or Upanishads, are summaries that form the doctrinal basis of the Hindu religion. Schopenhauer praised them as "deep, original, sublime thoughts," and said, "Access to the Vedas is the greatest privilege this century may claim over all previous centuries."

Vow of poverty. The spiritual meaning: "Gives all and expects nothing." A vow usually taken by one who chooses to own no material property. Sometimes used to remind us we have no worth but our real worth as a soul.

W

Waldorf schools. These schools, based upon Rudolf Steiner's anthroposophy, emphasize preparing students for spiritual advancement.

Walk-in. A term coined by Ruth Montgomery in *Strangers Among Us* and used in *Threshold to Tomorrow* to designate a change of souls in the same incarnation–allowed to occur due to a spiritual work or timely message on behalf of humanity.

Warrior. Esoterically, one who enters into the conscious struggle between levels of self, light and darkness, good and evil, within one's own nature. The warrior is developing the strengths, qualities, and persistence needed to do battle with the DWELLER ON THE THRESHOLD. Every battle is preparation.

Watcher (also known as Silent Watcher). Spiritual guides of the worlds. Also, that part of eternal or divine life that never identifies with form and remains ever conscious of its divine nature. The eternal magnet which draws the separated self–the fallen spark–homeward along the path of return. A voluntary exile itself, it shows the pilgrim the way back to the Source and will not cease its efforts until the last day of this life cycle. Also, the Great Being who is head of Hierarchy, the most evolved being of a system or group. This Great One, whose radiance pervades the entire system over which this Watch is extended, provides the home for innumerable beings. Lofty though the Great Being's surveillance may be, in every case an even Greater Being encompasses to an even greater extent.

Water mysteries. The gentle, emotional teachings of love, appreciation, respect, consideration, and esteem–centered around ADVENT, the birth of the Christ (Christmas), and EPIPHANY to aid in the development of the positive emotions in the astral body. As these are lifted to higher frequencies of the astral, they will in time blend with the mind/mental nature in TRANSMUTATION to become love-wisdom.

Wayshower. A prophet or enlightened one who by virtue of evolutionary progress can lead humanity through spiritual development. Master Jesus serves as the Wayshower for those on the Christian pathway. Each wayshower provides a pattern for those dedicated to follow toward self-realization and expression of the divine within.

Wedding garment. In the Christian mystery tradition, the radiant Light formed through purification of the astral and mental natures as we approach soul infusion. This transmuted subtle body must be developed before we can stand in the presence of the Christ or become a Christed One. This garment of the soul is the sublimated essence of the physical body together with the spiritualized forces of the etheric sheath: an ETHERIC BODY capable of functioning on the physi-cal and etheric planes without a physical body.

Wesak. A festival said to occur in the Himalayas at the full Moon of Taurus in which all members of the planetary hierarchy are present for a special blessing bestowed by the BUDDHA as he renews his bond with the work of planet Earth. The blessing is accepted for the planet by the Christ as head of HIERARCHY and then distributed to humanity through the MASTERS.

Western Yoga. *See* Yoga.

"What goes around comes around." A reference to the law of karma – inevitably just.

"When the student is ready, the teacher appears." Here we confront the realization that indeed the higher PLAN withholds until we have advanced enough within to realize the richness of the opportunity at hand. We may have to go through an agonizing process of breaking through our own barriers (usually not acknowledged) before we are ready, in position, and at a level of consciousness to appreciate the answer/teacher that brings solution. *See* Yoga, Krishna.

Whirling dervishes. Members of a sect of Islamic traditional mystics who use movement and dance to alter the consciousness. They are known to whirl in a circle for long periods of time as they enter the altered state and afterwards to continue with meditation and contemplation.

White magic. Specific acts of goodness done for the purpose of higher consciousness through affirmation, prayer, visualization, meditations, and "how-to" techniques. Acts must be unselfish, of positive benefit, and with good intent. Magic is an earlier word for "alchemy" and now "transformation."

Wholeness. An integration of the personality vehicles: physical, emotional, and mental natures are now ready for the spiritual self to lead the way toward higher consciousness–holiness.

Wicca. The Anglo-Saxon root of "witch," the European shamanistic tradition. Many contemporary witches of all varieties use this term as a less misunderstood word for "witchcraft."

Wiccan. A practitioner of the religion of Wicca or witchcraft. Technically applied only to British traditionalist witches, but widely used as a synonym for "witch."

Will. The Ray 1 quality of focused spiritual power that initiates action. The energy of ignited will creates action, often resulting in leadership. Ray 1's color is generally accepted as red. It is labeled as masculine.

Will-to-good. An Agni term. One of the qualities of Ray 1 energy directed specifically to the "Common Good," an oft-used term for higher will or God's will.

Wisdom. An advanced level of comprehension. Steps taught in spiritual understanding are: information (data and concepts), knowledge (use of), and wisdom (the ability to synthesize, to see spiritual relationships). The dedicated observation and practice of knowledge result in wisdom.

Wisdom teachings. A collection of wisdom; a body of knowledge about the hidden nature of humanity and the world held sacred through all time. The purpose of studying wisdom teachings is to attain such knowledge in the intellect as may be contemplated and to awaken the spiritual memory of the soul held within the COLLECTIVE UNCONSCIOUS of humanity.

Wise Guardians. Those from inner worlds who watch human progress, guiding and guarding as

197

they can without interfering with humanity's free will.

Wise Ones. A common title signifying those trained in the wisdom of the esoteric; certain Masters, saints, and sages in the Western tradition, and gurus in the East. High initiates who step down the scheme of evolution to the less evolved.

Witch. One who worships the Goddess in an Earth religion. Magic is part of the tradition – learning to work with forces of nature, following the disciplines of Witchcraft. Both male and female practitioners are called "witches."

Witchcraft. The most common practice of Neo-Paganism. A magical Earth religion with many traditions derived from various cultural sources around which covens and individual practitioners converge. Modern witchcraft traditions include Gardnerian, Alexandrian, Dianic, Celtic, Circle, Faerie, Shamanic, etc.

Witness consciousness. An impersonal level of awareness created through objectivity and spiritual insight and a developed chosen perspective from which we observe life at work.

Word, the creative. The sacred word from the ancient Sanskrit is said to be *Om,* deemed to be the generative first word or tone that vibrated through the receptive void to shape and maintain creation. This keynote went forth from the Creator to set creation, as we know it, into motion. Considered the sum of all vibrations of the universe, *Om* is the sound of God heard in meditation, the witness of a divine presence, the sacred word that was with God. Just as the *Om* issued forth from God to create all that is, the OM restores God's presence within creation. Thus it is an especially effective POWER WORD as a MANTRA.

Workers in the field of religion. A particular category of world servers who work through head, heart, and solar plexus to step down the higher plan for humanity.

Working "as if." A self-explanatory technique for aiding perception from an other-than-personal perspective. Working "as if" provides an opportunity to see if a given circumstance may be made feasible–a learning process to reveal what is advantageous and what is not.

World servers. Those in all arenas of life and service who willingly play their part in the divine Plan, seeking to further the work of the HIERARCHY and dedicated to the well-being of humanity. While working in the outer world, they maintain a deep, inner life from which they can draw all that is needed for active, spiritual work. Also called the NEW GROUP OF WORLD SERVERS, this company provides a training ground and a field of experience for those who choose to grow in spiritual stature and to ready themselves for active, directed service to the Christ. They can be categorized as: telepathic communicators, trained observers, magnetic healers, educators of the new age, political organizers, workers in the field of religion, scientific servers, psychologists, financiers and economists, and creative workers *(see individual definitions),* according to the teachings of MASTER DJWHAL KHUL. It is said that these function to satisfy the needs of humanity and to promote the development of the chakra system of the world servers.

World teacher. Christ is the world teacher – not Jesus, as the Christian tradition teaches, but the Great Lord Christ – teacher of angels and of humanity. He is known in the Orient as the BODHISATTVA, as Lord MAITREYA, and the one looked for by the devout Muslim as Imam Madhi. To this one is committed the guidance of humanity and the development of each human, the realization that the spark of God resides within. The world teacher is charged to develop that inner presence so each will know he or she is the son or daughter of the Most High.

Worry stone. Small pebbles used in the Huna system for invoking spiritual power, especially employed in rites of healing or the saying of affirmations.

Y

Yearning to perceive. An Agni expression. A great desire to know, to connect with the innate consciousness, and to proceed on the path of evolution is held within each. Often called DIVINE DISCONTENT.

Yeman-Yah. The divine black Mother. The universal Mother speaks, saying, "I show myself to those of my people as they can perceive. To those who need form, I am the mother of the peoples of the plains, forests, rivers, mountains, deserts, and of the nomads. To those who need no form, I am the Light from which all form proceeds." Seven rays flow from her head. Seven strands make up her collar of seven different metals. Rays flow to Earth from her heart and from her hands, unceasingly blessing her children of the Earth.

Yesod. This ninth sephirah on the kabalistic Tree of Life equates with the term "foundation" and is understood as that which is held in the unconscious depths of mind.

Yetzirah. A Chaldean term denoting the formative world. In kabalistic tradition the third of four lower worlds emanating from the seven lower sephiroth. Compares to the astral or psychological world.

Yin/yang. An Eastern designation for feminine and masculine energy, yin being female and yang being male. The symbol depicts the goal of balance of these energies.

Yod Hey Vod Hey (YHWH). In the Kabalah, the Tetragrammaton, the name of the One Almighty God.

Yoga

From the Sanskrit *yug,* meaning "union." The realization of union of spirit and matter (soul and personality) leading to the realization of at-one-ment. Also, various schools or systems which aim at union through spiritual exercises, practices, and meditation. Popularly refers to Hatha Yoga which emphasizes physical training but is only one of many yoga systems.

A yoga, or technique for union of personality and soul, emerges on a certain RAY influence. Over the centuries, some approaches survive and flourish even when the major influence of the time period changes with the needs of humanity. *Therefore, with the exception of Agni Yoga (the most modern), the yogas listed below are in order according to Ray. Agni Yoga is a synthesis of all rays but especially compatible to Rays 1 and 7, bridging will and orderliness as we move into a Ray 7 age.*

Agni Yoga. A modern school of thought emphasizing the everyday practice of ethical living, devotion, and purification of the physical, emotional, and mental bodies, aiding the process of synthesis. This modern path utilizes the practice of meditation to connect with the inner self and the work of clearing GLAMOURS and ILLUSIONS. The formation and application of a living ethic and the development of virtues within the personality characterize this still-emerging yoga practice or spiritual lifestyle associated with the birth of a new age in human history. Each practitioner works at his or her own pace, using a series of themes rather than rigid disciplines.

Raja Yoga. A system of yoga typified by development of psychic and spiritual powers and union with the higher self through will and spiritual intellect. A practical and experimental approach involving the exercise, regulation, and concentration of thought. Known as the "royal yoga" because of its high ethical standards and its goals to master the mental sub-planes and to link one's higher nature with the higher world, achieving realization of or oneness with the Soul. A Ray 1 approach, utilizing a code of honor and integrity, invoking will as a principal tool.

Kriya Yoga. A style of yoga related to Ray 1, similar to raja and karma yogas; will is invoked with specific disciplines to be added and subtracted from daily life. *See* Yogananda.

Karma Yoga. This system of yoga emphasizes the practice of service, work, and the fulfillment of duty, without attachment to selfish interest or expectations regarding the results of our labor. As a path of discipline or action, the aspirant uses will and wisdom in order to comprehend the law of cause and effect and the creation of effects. Selflessness and union with God are achieved through consecrated action and alignment with the high self. The karma yogi chooses carefully the seeds to plant (or set into motion). Also related to Ray 1.

Krishna Yoga is based on the *Bhagavad Gita* and is a Ray 2 approach of love-wisdom of the Krishna school of consciousness. Two great truths are used as guidelines: to love without ceasing and to remember many have become great through doing their duty without personal desire. Teaches the belief in being in a place for a reason, and that WHEN THE STUDENT IS READY, THE TEACHER WILL APPEAR. Fulfillment of duty is seen as a prerequisite for discipleship.

Jnana Yoga. Jnana means "wisdom," and this Ray 3 system of yoga emphasizes wisdom or true knowledge. Primarily a philosophical or intellectual school of yoga that seeks union with God through the path of discerning the real from the unreal. The power of the intellect is used to gather knowledge which, with love, is used for the benefit of all. Often considered theology and philosophy.

Hatha Yoga. This yoga system consists chiefly of physical postures (ASANAS) and exercises to keep the body fit and to influence the relationship between spirit and matter. In Sanskrit *ha* means "Sun" and *tha* means "Moon"–hence, the uniting of Sun and Moon, the physical and the etheric bodies, or balancing the male and female currents in the body. A Ray 4 healing technique.

Western Yoga. A set of prescribed exercises descending to modern times through the Zoroastrian-Mideast, designed for the more sensitive etheric bodies of modern disciples. Said to have been presented to the fifth ROOT RACE so disciples could anchor the intense energy with which they would connect without harm. Similar to calisthenics, the exercises are vigorous in nature, peppy, and with controlled, counted breaths–Ray 4 in nature. Brought to and taught in the U.S. by author and teacher Peter Roche de Coppens.

Laya Yoga. This system of yoga involves the development of the centers of the etheric body. Also called kundalini yoga or the yoga of energy, laya yoga is an advanced technique that requires close guidance by an experienced teacher. The purpose of this yoga path is to unfold and harmonize the etheric centers and to awaken the kundalini force in order to contact higher levels of consciousness. The cultivation of phenomena or altered states of consciousness in the Hindu tradition. A Ray 5 spiritual science approach designed to produce nonphysical, nonscientific results.

Kundalini Yoga. A Western variance to the laya school of yoga. Again, Ray 5 in nature and designed specifically to facilitate an advantageous arousal of the kundalini.

Siddha Yoga. Related to laya yoga, the teaching of awakening psychic abilities and the development of extended sense awareness, called "siddhas." TRANSCENDENTAL MEDITATION (TM) is the registered name for this Ray 5 approach established by Maharishi Mahesh Yogi in the United States in the 1960s.

Bhakti Yoga. A Ray 6 yoga system that aims at union with God through the practice of love and devotion. A natural pathway for those whose spiritual orientation is primarily devotional. This yoga utilizes the desire to love and worship the divine and to surrender to God's will and compassion. A particular saint, Master, or teacher is often used as a point of focus for adoration of the One God manifest in all forms. One's lover can become that focus as to be "one with the god within another."

Tantric Yoga. Literal meaning is "loom." A spiritual school of yoga in the Hindu tradition that uses the sexual energy within humanity as its transformational emphasis. While the approach generally begins with two partners, once understood, the discipline can be performed alone. An ecstasy experience created by bringing energy to the head centers is the goal, rather than releasing sexual fluids. Practiced as a path to enlightenment. This powerful Ray 6 yoga needs to be practiced under the guidance of an experienced and knowledgeable teacher as a protective measure.

Mantra Yoga. This particular practice uses affirmations, chants, words, and prayers to increase the connection to God and to experience the Holy Presence. This yoga system utilizes sound, or vibration, to affect matter, body, emotions, and mind. Based on the science of sound, specific mantras are used to create forms, manipulate matter, and control the energies of nature and of the self. In its most sacred form it is used as a powerful tool for the expansion of consciousness to further the evolution of humanity. This school of yoga seeks union with the divine through the use of mantras to increase the power of worship and adoration by releasing the God-self within each person, making each more sensitive to higher energies. Mantra Yoga is considered a Ray 7 approach.

Integral Yoga. The method delivered to the world through the teachings of Sri AUROBINDO.

Solar Yoga. A yoga technique named, developed, and taught by Master Omraam Mikhael Aïvinov that all yogas are contained in the sun, that we draw our energy from the sun and, through meditation, we unite ourselves with the spirit of the Christ which dwells within the Sun. Those who practice the discipline of witnessing the sunrise find a source of awe and inspiration for thought, meditation, and prayer; they find in the Sun the strength to live their daily lives in harmony and the courage and will to transform themselves. Once having achieved divine knowledge through meditation, we are never the same. Knowing even a few aspects of the truth, we are enabled to help others.

Yoga Sutras of Patanjali. Said to be both the text book for the inner schools and the most ancient of all the yogas, also known as the ancient teachings of RAJA YOGA.

Yogananda, Swami Paramahansa. b. India, 1893, d. 1952. Great spiritual teacher of the KRIYA YOGA lineage. He immigrated to the United States as a young man and founded the Self-Realization fellowship. He taught that the key to liberation is in the arousal of the KUNDALINI energy by meditation. His ancient meditation techniques were confirmed by modern scientific discoveries about energy and the functioning of the brain. *Autobiography of a Yogi,* 1946.

"You are Gods." We are reminded in the Old and New Testaments that we are Gods; the FEMININE PRINCIPLE of life, the soul, is to bring this about through the birth of the Christ within each.

Younger kingdoms. The mineral, plant, and animal kingdoms. They are considered to be younger than humanity in consciousness.

Z

Zen. A discipline of meditation practiced under the direction of a Zen master. This is considered an ACTIVE MEDITATION, rather than PASSIVE.

Zen bench. A low, wooden bench designed to support the body in a kneeling position and with an erect spine; considered beneficial to bring about a relaxed state for meditation.

Zendo. An ashram wherein Zen practitioners live a life of spiritual discipline.

Zodiac. A band of the celestial sphere that represents the path of the principal planets, Moon, and Sun of our solar system extending about eight degrees to either side of the ecliptic. According to the tropical zodiac, this band is divided into twelve parts called "signs," each of which is thirty degrees wide

and bears the name of the constellation for which it originally was named. The zodiac provides a systematic arrangement of the twelve astrological influences that affect all of evolving humanity. Thus personality types are determined by birth sign. In esoteric philosophy planetary position provides insights to the rhythms, strengths, and weaknesses of the inner nature. *See* Astrology.

Zodiacal archangel. A spiritual archetype for the Great Being who steps down the influences of each CELESTIAL HIERARCHY to the world of lower vibrations or lesser intelligences.

Zodiacal trinity. The three major astrological influences acting upon an individual, according to the sign in which the Sun, Moon, and ascendant are positioned in the natal chart. Establishes goals to be achieved for the growth of the personality in this lifetime.

Zoroaster. Greek name for Zarathustra, a Persian prophet of c. 600 B.C., who sought to abolish pagan religious practices and initiate a new morality. Zoroastrianism, the oldest living religion in the world, seeks to uphold two principles: to maintain life and to combat evil. Ahura-Mazda and his angels and archangels struggle against evil, Ahriman, his demons and archfiends. It teaches a heavenly journey of the SOUL, a belief in a heavenly book of record, bodily resurrection, and a paradise. Its sacred scriptures are contained in the *Avesta*, a collection of hymns, which in relating stories of the creation are strikingly similar to the Old Testament. The teachings of the *Avesta* were said to be revealed to Zoroaster while he meditated.

Zoroastrianism. A great temple religion which preserved ancient wisdom teachings six centuries before the birth of Jesus. The three Magi are believed to be mystics and astrologers of the Zoroastrian tradition. Zoroastrianism continues today among those known as the Parsees (or Parsis).

A Contemporary Mystery School

Your role in the Aquarian Age

The decade of the 1990s is one of personal and planetary struggle from which we move into a new era of enlightenment. Those who learn how to live ethical lifestyles–of service to the Hierarchy–are fundamental to this momentous transition.

Some seek to serve as counselors, ministers, or teachers. Regardless of vocation, if you learn to live consciously in service to the planet and the divine Plan, your life benefits the planet. Like a pebble dropped into a still pond, your intentions ripple in subtle yet utterly powerful ways each day. Helping to heal and transform your community, your life becomes a ministry, your place of work a temple. And you lead others by example.

All of this is the nature of spiritual leadership in the Aquarian Age. If you seek preparation to better serve in this way and would like to associate with others of like mind, here is an opportunity.

What the school offers–and why

Many have prophesied that mystery schools would reappear in the Aquarian Age. Their purpose is to train initiates in preparation for the externalization of the Hierarchy.

Sancta Sophia Seminary was established in 1978 to provide a one-of-a-kind, esoteric spiritual education. Five levels of off-campus and residential programs are offered. They provide deep understanding. As well, candidates who wish to become counselors, spiritual healing practitioners, ministers, or teachers of the Ageless Wisdom can earn certification. In Christianity, the Ageless Wisdom is offered through the esoteric tradition.

The story behind the school and its founder

In 1980, Sancta Sophia's dean, Carol E. Parrish, was revealed to the greater public by author Ruth Montgomery, in the best-selling *Threshold to Tomorrow*. The book elaborated upon Carol's remarkable psychic and spiritual abilities, and it described her role as a messenger in the new age.

Soon thereafter, Carol was guided by her Master to move the school from Florida to a place of greater safety during Earth changes and other tribulations. She was led to a specific, remote location in the beautiful Ozark Mountains of eastern Oklahoma to build Sancta Sophia.

Today, in addition to her personal teaching of Sancta Sophia students, Carol oversees all seminary classes and advisors. She continues to minister and publish widely acclaimed books and audiocassette programs. She is a highly sought international speaker.

Spiritually charged location enhances growth

The magnificent, wooded, 400-acre mountain top setting where Carol was inspired to build Sancta Sophia is also the home of the respected intentional community, Sparrow Hawk Village.

The village is a harmonious environment of fifty homes, office buildings and church. It has lovely gardens, good drinking water, and a sophisticated infrastructure. Villagers are self-supporting people who live, learn, meditate, and worship together.

Most important, the church sanctuary is centered on a vortex of special energies created by a star-shaped convergence of Earth ley lines. This creates a unique enclosure of spiritual energies which enhances the synergy of living, learning, and personal growth for every Sancta Sophia student. The village is a sacred space which helps those who visit to heal and make their lives whole. The spiritual vortex creates an environment for the training of initiates and preparation for the externalization of the Hierarchy.

How the program creates personal transformation

Whether an off-campus or a residential program is chosen, the emphasis behind every student's program is the unique, transformational process guided by master teacher, Dean Carol E. Parrish.

The process is synergistic. It starts with a format of meaningful home study and meditation techniques tailored to your personal goals. Month by month an individually assigned advisor is your spiritual mentor, using telephone sessions or personal meetings, or communicating by mail. The entire process catalyzes during periodic class weeks as you visit and enjoy the spiritually charged atmosphere at Sparrow Hawk Village.

210

Five levels of certification available

The distinctive process of home study, meditation, spiritual mentoring, and periodic classes at the village prepares the student to serve the divine Plan and the planet in one of five paths.

First, Practitioners gain legal certification as well-prepared lay ministers in counseling, spiritual healing, or teaching. Second, Teachers of Esoteric Philosophy are educators for the new paradigms of spirituality now emerging around the planet. Third, Ordination prepares ministers in Esoteric Christianity to bring the true Ageless Wisdom into metaphysical and mainstream churches of the world. Ordinations are endorsed by the International Council of Community Churches. Membership in this post-denominational, ecumenical Christian organization assists our ministers to bridge effectively to mainstream, exoteric Christianity.

Additionally, the graduate school offers two levels of certification to a limited enrollment. For students with the requisite background, commitment, and high creativity, Carol assists in designing programs leading to one of several Master's or Doctoral Degrees.

All programs are very reasonable in cost.

How to get more information

Do you seek to serve as a spiritual healing practitioner, minister, counselor, or teacher? Or, do you wish an advanced degree? If so, Sancta Sophia programs can prepare you to participate in the work of the Hierarchy as a spiritually awakened leader as we enter the modern era of enlightenment.

If you are interested in more information, you are invited to call the Registrar at (918) 456-3421, or write to Sancta Sophia Seminary, 11 Summit Ridge Drive–Dept. 26, Tahlequah, OK 74464. If you wish, request the name of the affiliated center, church, or class nearest you. Or, send in the order form at the end of this book.

"This book is a must for anyone doing dreamwork."

Richard Grams
The Leading Edge Review

"Among the many books which offer insight into the meaning of dream symbols, I find Ms. Tanner's to be the most approachable and useful, especially for beginning and intermediate explorers on this path."

H. Roberta Ossana, editor
Dream Network Journal

THE MYSTICAL, MAGICAL, MARVELOUS WORLD OF DREAMS

Wilda B. Tanner

Here is a proven method for using dreams to heal, solve problems and attain guidance for health, wealth, happiness and understanding. This best-seller, now in its 7th printing, is written for the spiritual seeker from a philosophical perspective.

In the first section of her mystical, magical, marvelous book, Wilda explains such phenomena as lucid dreaming, ESP or precognitive dreams, death-and-dying dreams, past-life dreams and nightmares. She also offers valuable insights on how to recall, interpret and work with dream symbols. The second section of this comprehensive book features a 260-page glossary of dream symbols and interpretations, plus an extensive cross-referenced index.

Wilda's joy and enthusiasm are contagious and her teachings, while deeply meaningful, are couched in simple language suited to every age.

Wilda B. Tanner has taught dream interpretation throughout the United States and Canada and has also been a frequent radio and T.V. guest. She is an ordained minister, teacher and philosopher.

$14.95 / tradepaper / 380pp / ISBN 0-945027-02-8

• **To purchase this book, please use the enclosed order form** •

"What Joseph Campbell has done with myth and ritual at the cognitive level, Carol Parrish-Harra does at the practical level. This work is a milestone and a 'must' for any person wishing to understand the deeper psycho-spiritual aspects of the complex human personality."

Peter Roche de Coppens, Ph.D.
Internationally recognized author, lecturer and psychotherapist
Prof. of Sociology and Anthropology, East Stroudsburg Univ.

THE BOOK OF RITUALS
Personal and Planetary Transformation

Rev. Carol Parrish-Harra

You will benefit from the author's vast knowledge of astrology as you read about your specific sun sign and the "celestial hierarchy" associated with it. The author explains the exact challenges you face on your spiritual path and gives practical advice on how to open your physical and non-physical senses to effectively utilize the many subtle energies of the universe.

This highly original work presents specific rituals involving prayer, song, chanting, dance and meditation for each full moon period and for major festivals.

Reverend Carol Parrish-Harra, author of dozens of books and teaching tapes, has been identified by Ruth Montgomery as an Aquarian Age messenger. She is Dean of Sancta Sophia Seminary, founder and pastor of the Light of Christ Community Church and cofounder of Sparrow Hawk Village, an intentional spiritual community in Tahlequah, OK.

$14.95 / tradepaper / 280pp / ISBN 0-945027-10-9

• TO ORDER, PLEASE SEE THE LAST PAGE OF THIS SECTION •

*"A beautifully written book that under-
stands death and dying from the holistic
perspective of the New Age. It deserves a
wide audience; I highly recommend it."*

Dr. Kenneth Ring, Director
International Association for Near-Death Studies
Author, *Life After Death, Heading Towards Omega*

THE NEW AGE HANDBOOK ON DEATH AND DYING

Rev. Carol Parrish-Harra

Proven techniques for expanding and transforming painful views of death are offered in this profound book of life-affirming wisdom. These insights have evolved out of the author's ministries with terminally ill patients and their families, from her own near-death experience and from her grief following the sudden loss of her daughter and granddaughter.

Counselors, family members and friends alike will find this book to be an excellent source of guidance and comfort in helping others prepare for the death experience. Join with Reverend Parrish-Harra as she seeks to facilitate a better understanding of spiritual teachings concerned with death and affirm a stronger belief in a living Creator with a perfect plan.

*"...helps guide our hearts towards healing resolu-
tions...shines a light on grief, convincing us we can
face death, and learn and grow in the process."*

BettyClare Moffatt, author
Cofounder, Mothers of AIDS Patients

$10.95 / tradepaper / 196pp / ISBN 0-945027-09-5

• TO ORDER, PLEASE USE THE FORM WHICH FOLLOWS •

"A great book for beginners,

Doe has made bite-size pieces out of complex theory. Best of all, an astrology book that isn't intimidating!"

Carol E. Parrish-Harra, Ph.D.
Best-selling author and spiritual teacher
Dean, Sancta Sophia Seminary

DO YOU SPEAK ASTROLOGY?
Learn the Language of the Skies

Doe Donovan

This book will prove especially valuable to those just beginning to learn to speak "the language of the skies." Doe's lively conversational writing style shortens potentially lengthy explanations as she describes signs, planets and aspects. Her interpretations are fascinating and include the natal charts of many famous personalities, such as Johnny Carson, Marilyn Monroe, Madonna, Michael Jordan and General Norman Schwarzkopf.

Doe Donovan's extraordinary presentation of traditional astrology has generated a distinct and lucid teaching book. She has simplified the complex study of astrology in a great how-to manner, using a contemporary approach to a centuries-old subject.

Doe Donovan is a professional astrologer and has been a faculty member at the American Federation of Astrologers biennial conventions. She is also a frequent contributor for the AFA Journal. Her background includes ten years of teaching communications arts and graduate work in education.

$12.95 / tradepaper / 272pp / ISBN 0-945027-05-2

• TO ORDER THIS BOOK, PLEASE USE THE ENCLOSED FORM •

Spiritual Growth Books and Tapes

Please send the following books:

Quantity		Price each	Totals
_____	The Mystical, Magical, Marvelous World of Dreams – *a concise guide to dream interpretation*	$14.95	_____
_____	Do You Speak Astrology? – *great for astrology beginners*	$12.95	_____
_____	The Book of Rituals – *to create personal & planetary transformation*	$14.95	_____
_____	The New Age Handbook on Death and Dying – *excellent resource for comfort & guidance*	$10.95	_____
_____	The Gateway of Liberation – *classic writings on the Ageless Wisdom*	$10.95	_____
_____	The New Dictionary of Spiritual Thought – *1,100 definitions of Western and Eastern esoteric and spiritual concepts*	$14.95	_____

Please send the following teaching tapes by Carol E. Parrish-Harra:

		Price	Totals
	Adventure in Awareness – *Ageless Wisdom concepts & teachings*		
_____	I - Breadth of Esoteric Teachings	$60	_____
_____	II - Awakening Our Inner Consciousness	$60	_____
_____	III - Toward Deeper Self-Realization	$60	_____
_____	Meditation Plus – *12 meditation techniques for spiritual growth*	$30	_____
_____	Coming to the Sunrise – *advanced meditation for self-purification*	$25	_____
_____	Energy Ecstasy *(book used with "Sunrise" Tapes)*	$12.95	_____
_____	Healing – *realize your own healing potential & how to use it*	$30	_____
_____	New Age Christianity – *discover the Christ-within*	$30	_____
_____	Experience New Dimensions – *techniques for psychic development*	$35	_____
_____	The Aquarian Rosary (tape) – *stimulate heart & mind to greater love*	$12.95	_____
_____	The Aquarian Rosary (book)	$8.95	_____

☐ I am interested in knowing more about **Sancta Sophia Seminary.** Please send additional information.

Subtotal _____

Shipping and Handling ($2 first item, $1 each additional) _____

TOTAL ENCLOSED _____

Payment by: ☐ Check ☐ Visa ☐ MC

Card # _____ Exp. Date _____

Signature _____

Name _____

Address _____

_____ Daytime Phone _____

VILLAGE BOOK STORE
22 Summit Ridge Drive, Dept. 26
Tahlequah, OK 74464
For phone orders, please call (918) 456-3421
Quantity discounts available upon request

Contemporary Mystery School

I am interested in receiving information on the contemporary mystery school described on pages 193-195 of this book. I realize there is no obligation. Please send information to:

Name _____

Address _____

City, State, Zip _____

Telephone (_____) _____

Please detach and mail

BUSINESS REPLY MAIL

FIRST CLASS MAIL PERMIT NO. 11 TAHLEQUAH, OK

POSTAGE WILL BE PAID BY ADDRESSEE

Registrar
Sancta Sophia Seminary
11 Summit Ridge Drive-Dept. 26
Tahlequah, OK 74464-9904

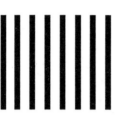